HERMÈS
PARIS

UN JARDIN
À CYTHÈRE

the sun as perfume

HOUSE OF FINN JUHL

Finn Juhl | 1953

The 77 Chair

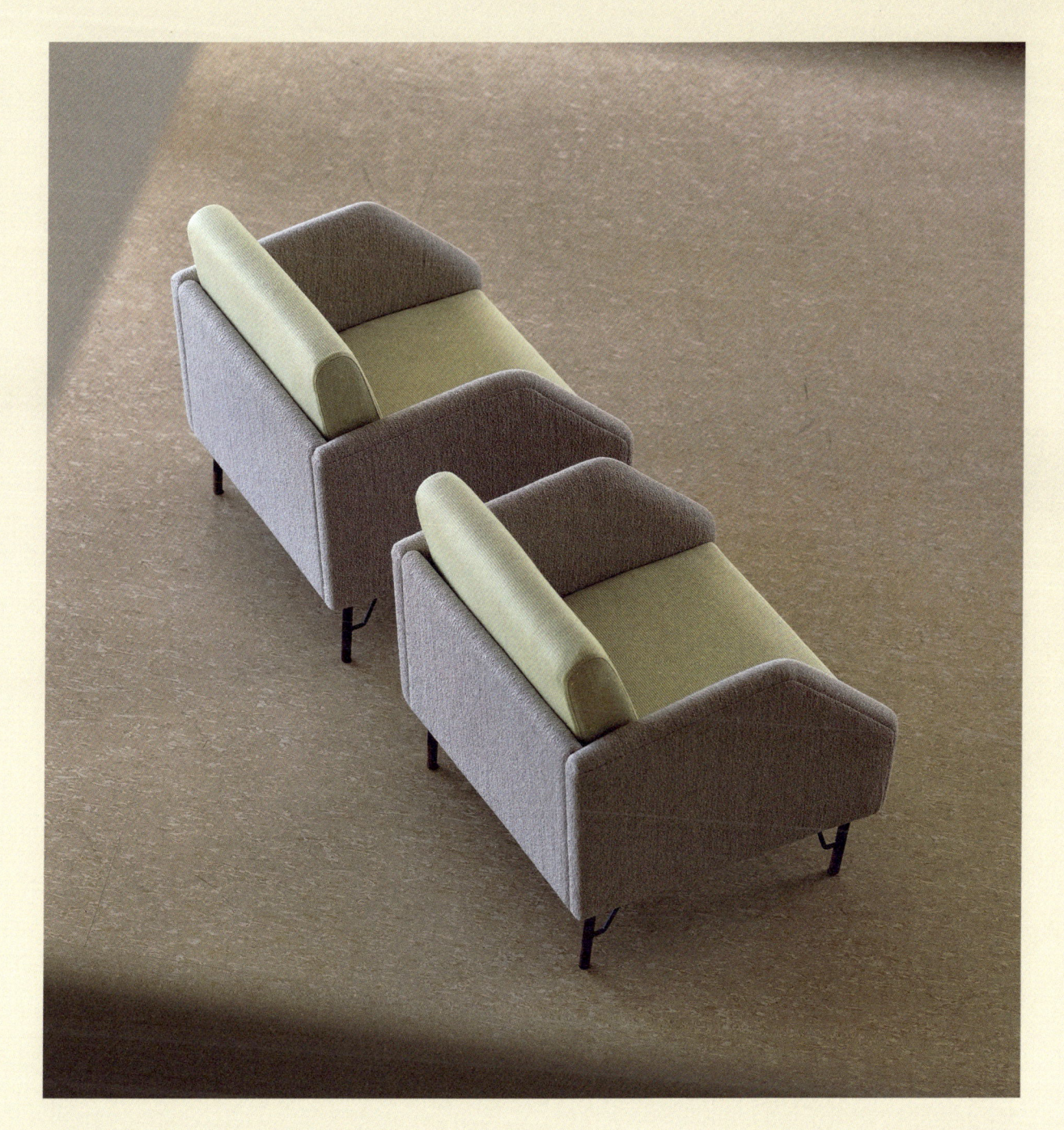

The 77 Chair upholstered in the textiles Fuse and Helia from Kvadrat.

Finn Juhl is renowned for his iconic furniture designs and for revolutionizing the Danish furniture tradition with his sculptural and artistic design language. However, with its refined and simple expression, the 77 Chair from 1953 is probably Finn Juhl's most atypical design as the graphic shape traces lineage back to the Bauhaus era. The chair evokes memories of the international airport lounges and hotel lobbies of the 50s and 60s.

Behind the rather modest exterior lies time-consuming craftsmanship and materials of the finest quality. The chair is crafted in Denmark on a solid blind frame, upholstered and hand-stitched, according to traditional craftsmanship in textile or leather. Read more at finnjuhl.com

Reform

Atelier Collection   Glass handles by Nina Nørgaard   reformcph.com

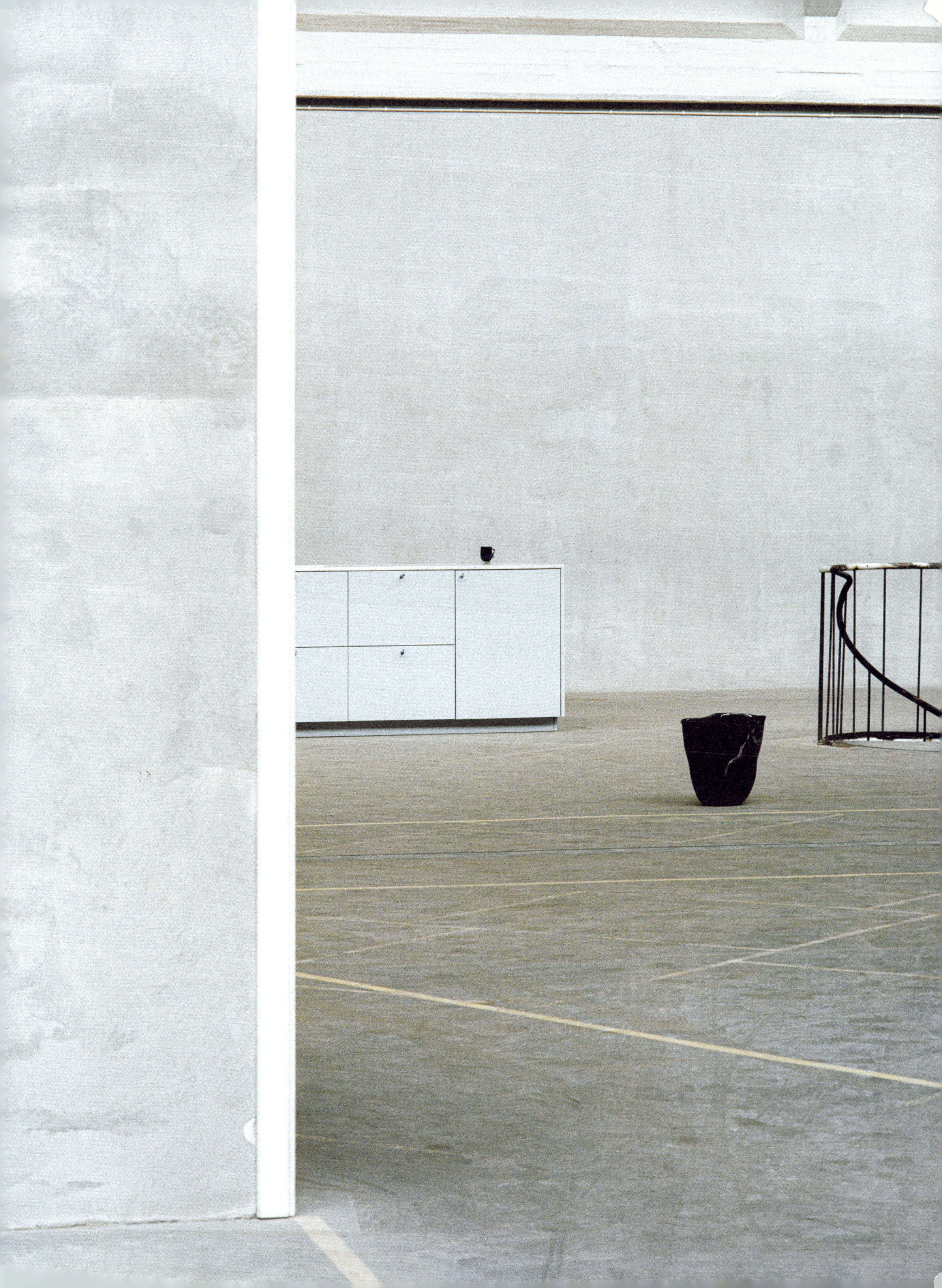

Eat Your Greens

Handmade Designs in Resin

tf

tf.design

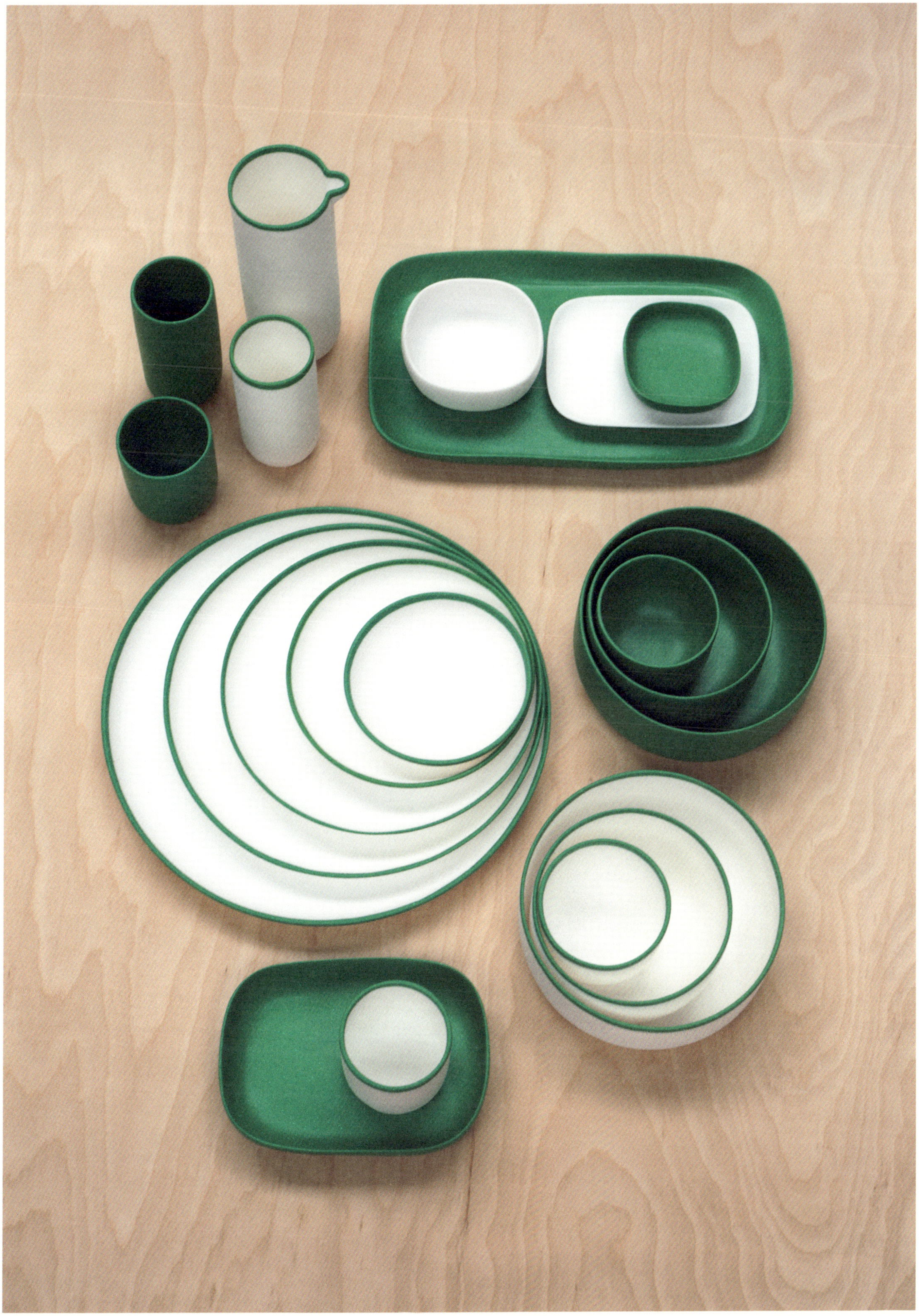

MASTHEAD

KINFOLK

MAGAZINE

EDITOR IN CHIEF — John Burns
ART DIRECTOR — Christian Møller Andersen
DESIGN DIRECTOR — Alex Hunting
COPY EDITOR — Rachel Holzman

STUDIO

PUBLISHING DIRECTOR — Edward Mannering
STUDIO & PROJECT MANAGER — Susanne Buch Petersen
DESIGNER & ART DIRECTOR — Staffan Sundström
DIGITAL MANAGER — Cecilie Jegsen

CROSSWORD — Mark Halpin
PUBLICATION DESIGN — Alex Hunting Studio
COVER PHOTOGRAPH — Zhong Lin

The views expressed in Kinfolk magazine are those of the respective contributors and are not necessarily shared by the company or its staff. Kinfolk (ISSN 2596-6154) is published quarterly by Ouur ApS, Amagertorv 14B, 2, 1160 Copenhagen, Denmark. Printed by Park Communications Ltd in London, United Kingdom. Color reproduction by Park Communications Ltd in London, United Kingdom. All rights reserved. No part of this publication may be reproduced, distributed or transmitted in any form or by any means, including photocopying or other electronic or mechanical methods, without prior written permission of the editor in chief, except in the case of brief quotations embodied in critical reviews and certain other noncommercial uses permitted by copyright law. The US annual subscription price is $80 USD. Airfreight and mailing in the USA by WN Shipping USA, 156-15, 146th Avenue, 2nd Floor, Jamaica, NY 11434, USA. Application to mail at periodicals postage prices is pending at Jamaica NY 11431. US Postmaster: Send address changes to Kinfolk, WN Shipping USA, 156-15, 146th Avenue, 2nd Floor, Jamaica, NY 11434, USA. Subscription records are maintained at Ouur ApS, Amagertorv 14B, 2, 1160 Copenhagen, Denmark. SUBSCRIBE: Kinfolk is published four times a year. To subscribe, visit www.kinfolk.com/subscribe or email us at info@kinfolk.com. CONTACT US: If you have questions or comments, please write to us at info@kinfolk.com. For advertising and partnership inquiries, get in touch at advertising@kinfolk.com.

WORDS

Precious Adesina
Alex Anderson
Nana Biamah-Ofosu
Ed Cumming
Benjamin Dane
Stephanie d'Arc Taylor
Gabriele Dellisanti
Daphnée Denis
Marah Eakin
Suyin Haynes
Angela Hui
Elle Hunt
Robert Ito
Annabel Bai Jackson
Rosalind Jana
Tara Joshi
Liv Lewitschnik
Jenna Mahale
Alexandra Marvar
Emily May
Kabelo Sandile Motsoeneng
Emily Nathan
Okechukwu Nzelu
John Ovans
Caitlin Quinlan
Manju Sara Rajan
Debika Ray
Asher Ross
Charles Shafaieh
George Upton
Alice Vincent
Annick Weber

STYLING, SET DESIGN, HAIR & MAKEUP

Annie & Hannah
Kelly Fondry
Fuzai
Simone Henneberg
Sting Hsieh
Naomi Itkes
Juno Ko
Nick Lennon
Wendy Lux
Freya Ni
Anna Sundelin
Yu Ting Tung
Preston Wada
Carlee Wallace
Chen Yu
Zinn Zhou

ARTWORK & PHOTOGRAPHY

Thomas Albdorf
Luca Anzalone
Lauren Bamford
Maya Beano
Andoni Beristain
Peter Bogaczewicz
George Byrne
Valerie Chiang
Chiron Duong
Sebastián Faena
Kelly Geddes
Viggo Hasselquist
Cecilie Jegsen
Jaeha Kim
Kourtney Kyung Smith
Arianna Lago
Alixe Lay
Zhong Lin
Luke Lovell
Raphael Lucena
Christian Møller Andersen
Emman Montalvan
Anne Nowak
Sina Östlund
Nik Pate
Andrés Reisinger
Staffan Sundström
Florent Tanet
Armin Tehrani
Marsý Hild Þórsdóttir
Emma Trim
Xiaopeng Yuan

PUBLISHER

Chul-Joon Park

08   ISSUE FORTY-NINE

vipp

Swivel chair

VIPP.COM

ISSUE FORTY-NINE

WELCOME
Scandinavia Special

The media often exoticizes Scandinavia as a paragon of how life could be, conceptualizing some of its small, ordinary moments into lifestyle trends that might make our own days a bit brighter if we recreated them at home. We could enjoy a little more *hygge*, the Danish concept of coziness, for instance, or we might try *lagom*—the Swedish art of moderation. We can strive for *sisu*, Finland's stoic determination, or to integrate more Swedish *fika* (coffee breaks, but better) into our routines. Per the book *Norwegian Wood: Chopping, Stacking, and Drying Wood the Scandinavian Way*, we might even want to try log splitting.

For all of the comfort, civility or conviviality these terms invoke, they don't always travel well outside of the societies in which they originated—nor do they present a full picture of life within them. In Issue Forty-Nine, we meet with an all-star cast of illustrious cultural leaders who draw their creative strength from the darker side of Europe's northernmost reaches. On page 134, pop sensation Tove Lo explains how, as a teenager, she was prized in Sweden for writing stories "about a girl doing twisted things"—a skill that she's since scaled up for a global audience with her searingly honest songs that explore some of life's most troubling experiences. On page 146, writer Emily Nathan meets artist Karin Mamma Andersson at her Stockholm studio, scratching below the surface of her ostensibly gorgeous paintings to find something broken—a quality, Andersson confesses, that has brought more than one child to tears. And on page 166, we catch provocative filmmaker Ruben Östlund after he presided over the jury at the Cannes Film Festival, enmeshing himself among the elite that he relishes undermining in his movies. "I love when the stakes are socially dangerous," he says.

Elsewhere in the issue, we bring you stories of people striving for the things that would genuinely make life brighter and better for anyone, wherever they are. Hollywood actor Mamoudou Athie, star of the latest Pixar movie, has made the pursuit of more freedom his modus operandi; author Jenny Odell explains how she longs for more time; and choreographer Ryan Heffington shares why he's looking to strengthen his community.

Many of our other features examine the highs and lows of cultural production, including a Zhong Lin fashion editorial dedicated to the sartorial contributions of subculture, a longform essay investigating what happened to the mainstream, and shorter pieces on tackiness, plain aesthetics and why hotel art is so boring.

WORDS
JOHN BURNS

ENDURING
DESIGN

Lounge — Hans J. Wegner — From 1950

There is a masterful simplicity to Hans J. Wegner's designs. At Carl Hansen & Søn, we translate these timeless ideas into furniture that lasts a lifetime. Since 1950, we have worked with the finest natural materials to produce a wide range of pieces from Wegner's collection of lounge furniture. The goal is clear: to create furniture crafted to last through generations.

CARL HANSEN & SØN

Explore more at CARLHANSEN.COM
or visit your nearest Flagship Store

CONTENTS

18 — 48

STARTERS
On time, tackiness and freebies.

18	Word: Zeitgeber	34	Lease on Life
20	Checked Out	36	Tough Call
21	On the Cheap	37	Minor Lapses
22	Free Spirit	38	Pitch Perfect
24	Mimi Shodeinde	40	Marcio Kogan
26	Beauty in the Beat	44	Good Enough
28	The Pizza Effect	46	Nell Wulfhart
30	Reid Bartelme & Harriet Jung	48	How to Say No
32	Between the Ears	–	–

50 — 112

FEATURES
From mountains, cities and deserts.

50	Mamoudou Athie	84	At Work With Muller Van Severen
60	Hanging Out with Andy Baraghani	92	Mass Destruction
66	Studio Visit: Heidi Gustafson	96	Dancing with Ryan Heffington
74	Jenny Odell	104	A World of Difference

"It's beautiful to walk through life in the valley between reality and surrealism." (Ryan Heffington – P. 96)

12   ISSUE FORTY-NINE

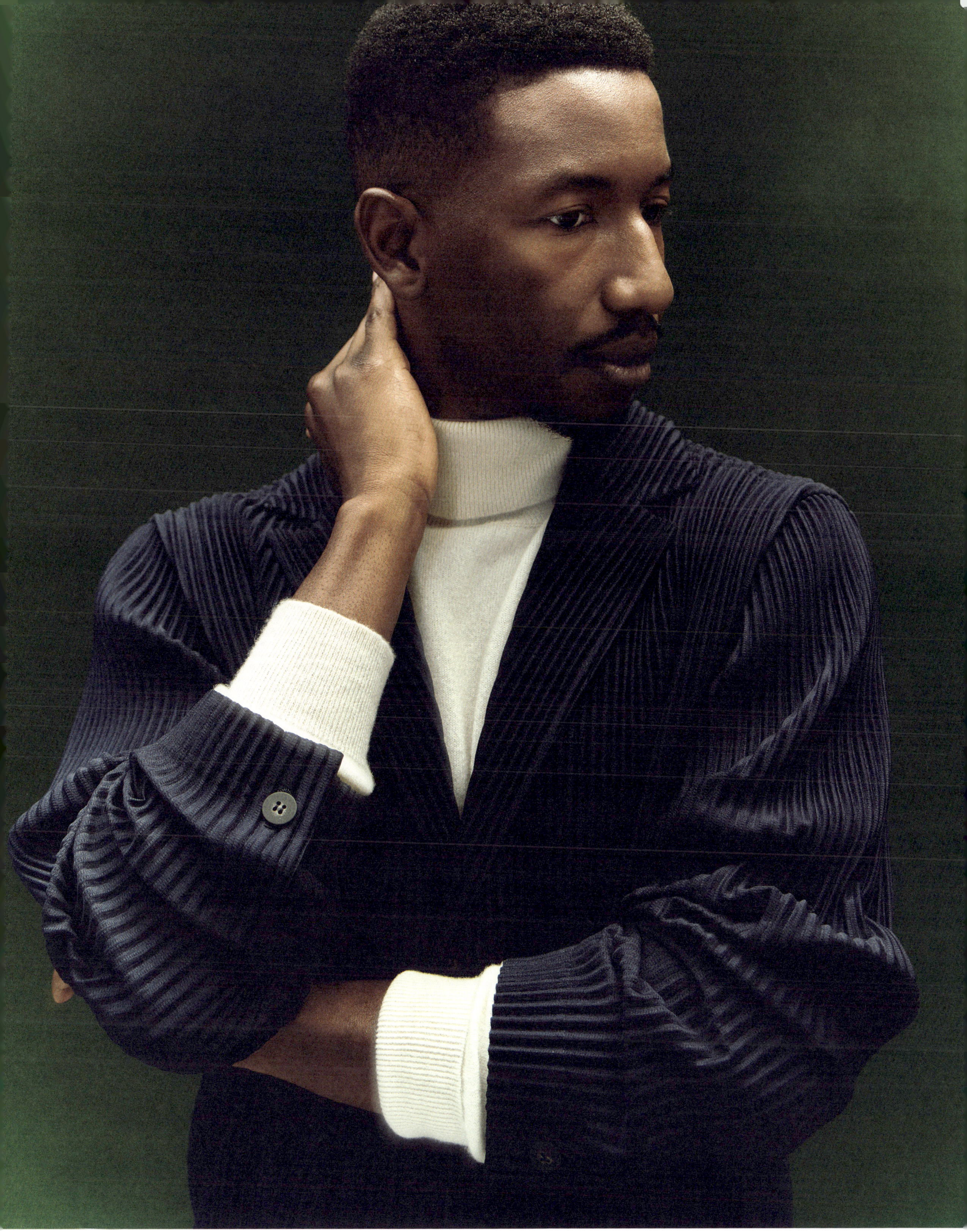

"I'm always very fascinated by how love can completely change a human being." (Tove Lo – P. 143)

CONTENTS

114 — 176

SCANDINAVIA
Meet the northern stars.

114	Urban Doom	146	Karin Mamma Andersson
126	Amalie Smith	158	Fares Fares
134	Tove Lo	166	Ruben Östlund

178 — 192

DIRECTORY
Art pop, audiobooks and clutter.

178	Object Matters	186	Cult Rooms
179	Last Night	188	Behind the Scenes
180	Róisín Murphy	190	Credits
182	Crossword	191	Stockists
183	Correction	192	My Favorite Thing

KINFOLK

marset
Taking care of light

Part 1.
STARTERS
A decision coach, hotel art & how to buy nothing.
18 — 48

18	Word: Zeitgeber
21	On the Cheap
22	Free Spirit
28	The Pizza Effect
36	Tough Call
40	Marcio Kogan
46	Nell Wulfhart

WORD: ZEITGEBER
A new treatise on time.

WORDS
DAPHNÉE DENIS
PHOTO
REISINGER STUDIO

Etymology: Zeitgeber literally translates from German as "time giver." The term was coined in the late 1950s by physician Jürgen Aschoff, a pioneer in the study of biological rhythms, or chronobiology. Aschoff established that humans and animals synchronize their circadian rhythms, meaning the cycles that command the body's internal clock, to the Earth's rotation. According to his research, our notion of time and the way our bodies adapt to it respond to zeitgebers—environmental time cues—such as sunlight or feeding cycles. In an experiment that lasted over two decades, from 1964 to 1989, Aschoff tested how volunteers responded to being cut off from those zeitgebers when isolated in a bunker for weeks at a time. His conclusion: Devoid of time cues, humans no longer had an internal clock and each individual developed zeitgebers of their own.

In her 2023 book, *Saving Time: Discovering a Life Beyond the Clock*, artist Jenny Odell proposes a new, 21st-century take on the word.[1] Our notion of time, she argues, is malleable and expands or shrinks following zeitgebers that can be as varied as a mother's breastfeeding cycle, an assistant organizing their time according to their boss's preferences or a Twitter user's ever-updating news feed.

Meaning: "Are you still watching?" Most Netflix subscribers will know—and dread—what this question implies. Namely, the realization that it's already been 90 minutes (roughly three episodes) since the moment they started watching a series on the platform. As hours dilute into a dopamine-filled storyline, a streaming-induced zeitgeber can take the form of how many episodes one can binge-watch at a time.

How we experience the passage of time is subjective, but so is the way our bodies and our brains adapt to it. Odell believes that capitalism and modern technologies can shape our perception of time just like dark-light cycles do. For instance, she says, she noticed how Twitter's nonstop notifications accelerated her own relationship to time passing. Living at the pace of outrage-fueled tweets and breaking news affected her interest in events that developed more slowly or "less sensationally," like the local effects of climate change, or even what happened in her friends' lives, she writes in *The New York Times*.

The same goes for someone who is accustomed to constant communication from their employer, or who has to wake up before dawn to commute to work. Through these artificial cues, our brains can be entrained into cycles that continue to influence our lives' patterns even after the original zeitgeber is gone. Odell was able to opt out of social media and readjust to a calmer life offline, but she warns against the lasting impact of modern society's frantic pace on our body clocks. While it's not always possible to do away with those external factors, awareness of what shapes our time allows us to slow down and focus on what really matters: our loved ones, our immediate environment and being in the moment.

(1) Odell is also the author of *How to Do Nothing: Resisting the Attention Economy*. She speaks to Robert Ito about the ideas behind both books on page 74.

The human experience known as travel might take place under any number of circumstances. Sometimes it's an activity intentionally pursued—think vacations, destination weddings or business trips—and sometimes it just happens, incidentally, when we pull into a motel on the way from point A to point B.

A good hotel will be designed to accommodate the mindset of the guests for whom it is intended, and hotel art has traditionally been used to help it accomplish that task. When Bob and Martha arrive in matching florals and head straight for their deluxe Mai-Tai Suite, they may not know that this particular roadside inn sits on an estuary, or that the local hot spot is a Domino's Pizza; in fact, they probably don't care. So their lodging confers the gift of the generic: algorithmically generated abstractions woven into low-pile carpets and walls adorned with aesthetic platitudes, like paintings of tree-lined streets or photographs of blossoming fields.

The foundational absence of substance, style, vision or voice has always defined the genre. Like the term "elevator music," "hotel art" is used as a descriptor with derogatory, dismissive intention. When it comes to hotel art, disappearance from the conscious plane —and total integration into the background —seems to be the benchmark for success.

There's a reason for this, of course. Throughout history, paid-for accommodation was primarily of the unregulated persuasion—bars with beds, in essence—where weary travelers could collapse and snag an hour of shut-eye before stumbling back out into the dawn. What distinguished these places from one another was nothing at all: Their defining characteristic was that they could be found precisely anywhere you happened to find yourself. And given that the hotel industry claims this as its origin story, it's easy to see why hotel art has traditionally avoided "place," with its inherent histories, characteristics and challenges. It has striven, instead, to make guests feel content, without noticing it—to offer an undefined pleasantness that has nothing to do with the world beyond the walls.

With time, hotel art has continued to evolve, and the supremely bland nature of its core sensibility has morphed into something just as recognizable, yet more palatable to a global demographic that craves the illusion of sophistication. Described in 2016 by the writer Kyle Chayka as "AirSpace," this visual geography is distinguished by a "faux-artisanal aesthetic" that virtue signals quality and elegance: minimalist furniture; textiles in varying shades of beige; and, almost without fail, industrial lighting.[1]

But our world is changing. Rather than offering a universe of mysteries to discover, it is now overrun by "places," each one geotagged for an eager audience—and hotel art is transforming into its own antithesis. Today, titans of contemporary art are flown in to design penthouse suites—Damien Hirst's absurdist contribution to the Las Vegas Palms Casino features a cantilevered pool and sharks suspended in formaldehyde—and iconic installations that operate as public monuments, like Dale Chihuly's shimmering reef of glass over the Bellagio's front desk. Hotel art has become the destination, one more meaningless pixel-drop in an endless sea of scrolling feeds. And the benign, respectfully anonymous territory embraced by those old lobby walls, that liminal space between somewhere and nowhere at all, seems to be gone for good.

(1) In an essay for *The Verge*, Chayka attributed the acceleration of the AirSpace aesthetic to companies such as Airbnb using technology to break down geography. "Even as it markets unique places as consumable goods," he wrote, "it helps its users travel without actually having to change their environment."

CHECKED OUT
Why is hotel art so boring?

WORDS
EMILY NATHAN
ARTWORK
ANNE NOWAK

There is a pink-tinted photo of food writer Nigella Lawson in a Playboy Bunny T-shirt, cocktail shaker in French-manicured hand, that I love. It opens a chapter in her cookbook *Nigella Bites* entitled "Trashy," in which she extols the virtues of watermelon daiquiris, fried peanut butter and banana sandwiches, and ham cooked in Coke. "I'm not interested in pleasing food snobs or purists," Lawson writes. "Surely there is a place … for a bit of kitsch in the kitchen."

Much of the current predilection for overt tackiness can be traced back to around the same time that *Nigella Bites* was published, the early 2000s. From the Y2K-inspired clothes to much-lauded books on British bubblegum pop and podcasts like Caroline O'Donoghue's *Sentimental Garbage*, which regularly stops off in the mid-aughts via Avril Lavigne and *America's Next Top Model*, we seem to be in the fevered, nostalgic grip of an era when mass communication, celebrity culture, reality TV and Juicy Couture exploded.

Trashy. Kitsch. Vulgar. Gaudy. Tacky. Each word possesses its own complicated meaning, but clustered together they catch the current cultural moment. Over the last half decade, there has been a renewed emphasis on the virtues of banal and so-called "bad" taste. Like Lawson, its devotees wish to reclaim their joys back from the snobs. In 2021, American writer Rax King published *Tacky: Love Letters to the Worst Culture We Have to Offer*—an essay collection exploring the author's lowbrow passions, from the cosmetic (frosted lip gloss, vanilla body mist) to the pop-cultural (Meat Loaf, *Jersey Shore*). "As far as I'm concerned, tackiness is joyfulness," she argues. "To be proudly tacky, your aperture for all the too-much feelings—angst, desire, joy—must be all the way open." King's essays are often anchored in her own coming-of-age in the early aughts: Tackiness becomes entangled with memory, with the growing pains of moving toward adulthood and entering the world of taste, culture and social mores.

I'm not sure if I would have loved this photo of Nigella Lawson several years ago. It now comes with a veneer of so-bad-it's-good cool, the right sprinkling of ironic magic. Tackiness may require unabashed love, but it also rewards those who get the references—and the current mood. As Karl Lagerfeld once proclaimed, "Trendy is the last stage before tacky." The tack-o-meter is constantly adjusting. It moves with the times, chewing up the past to recalibrate our present tastes.

WORDS
ROSALIND JANA
PHOTO
JAEHA KIM

ON THE CHEAP
The greatness of cultural worsts.

KINFOLK

FREE SPIRIT
A primer on the gifting economy.

"Find your abundance mindset. Give away or ask for anything you want." This is the inspiring, sweeping slogan of the Buy Nothing Project, an online community committed to exchanging free stuff among local people that was founded in 2013. A few decades into the internet era, the distribution of our excess resources online is a familiar concept: A similar platform, the Freecycle Network was founded a decade earlier in 2003; Gumtree, Craigslist and Facebook Marketplace are all full of people off-loading their unwanted possessions.

The Buy Nothing Project built on these concepts, but its founders, Liesl Clark and Rebecca Rockefeller, had loftier ideals: not only to be a means of exchanging goods, but to be a hyperlocal social movement that would ultimately create stronger bonds and encourage a spirit of generosity. "We exist to build resilient communities where our true wealth is the connections forged between neighbors," its website states, before claiming 7.5 million members across 128,000 communities around the world.

Clark and Rockefeller also differentiated the platform from other networks in that it encouraged requests, not just offers, and that it wanted to make people feel good about whatever they had to give—however bizarre. "Literally, we want people to come in and offer their onion skins and their chunks of concrete," Rockefeller once told the magazine *Wired*. Today, the things people exchange range from the usual furniture pieces and household items to the unexpected (breast milk, a rug covered in dog poop) to the seemingly useless (a half-eaten pizza and dryer lint).[1]

Like many idealistic social projects, as the Buy Nothing Project has grown, it has attracted criticisms. Some are predictable: Of course, it won't solve poverty and the environmental crisis on its own; it doesn't tackle the underlying structural causes of inequality; online groups predicated on personal interactions always run the risk of becoming monoculture or exclusionary. Other critiques are more practical: The exchange of regulated items, such as medicines or safety equipment, is potentially dangerous.

What is perhaps more interesting is that, through this prism of formal exchange, seemingly worthless commodities are magically finding value—the lint and pizza remnants are just the tip of the iceberg. Are we simply incapable of resisting the urge to consume? Or is there something about the notion of "free" that encourages a tendency to hoard? After all, there's no limit to how much free stuff you can afford.

At the opposite end of the spectrum is the kind of mindful consumption encouraged by the craft movement: objects produced in small batches, thoughtfully—often by hand—and usually given quite high prices to reflect the labor and materials. Such prices force people to think twice about buying, but also exclude anyone who can't afford them.

There is no doubt that we have, on this planet now, more stuff than we will ever need, making any attempt to curb excessive production and encourage a mindful approach to consumption worthwhile. Making ethical choices should be an option for everyone, regardless of means. And whether free or consciously expensive, it's clear that price is rarely an indicator of value—it's simply a way of signaling our own priorities. The methods we choose matter little, as long as we start by asking if we need something at all.

WORDS
DEBIKA RAY
PHOTO
LUCA ANZALONE

(1) Dryer lint can serve many useful purposes: As hamster bedding, as package filler and—when stored inside a toilet paper tube—as a fire starter. Failing that, it's also biodegradable and can be put on a compost pile.

MIMI SHODEINDE

WORDS
NANA BIAMAH-OFOSU
PHOTO
ALIXE LAY

An audience with the architect.

Mimi Shodeinde is challenging preconceived ideas about African design. In London, her design and interior architecture studio, Miminat Designs, is developing its own particular language—one characterized by rich material palettes, and based on her intuition. "My intention is to produce design that speaks to my journey as a British Nigerian," she says. "I want to express my culture in my work."

NANA BIAMAH-OFOSU: How do you imagine people living with your work?

MIMI SHODEINDE: I want people to feel proud, and for it to afford them a feeling of home as a sanctuary. I appreciate how fortunate I've been to have clients who are in the position to spend the amount that they do on my work, and I want them to be fully immersed in the experience of my objects, furniture and spaces.

NBO: What would you say is central to that experience?

MS: History and heritage play a big role in establishing a visual language, but the most important factor is character. That's what creates beautiful things in this world. It's central to everything that I do.

NBO: Some of your earlier objects are named in Yoruba. What does it mean to give your work Nigerian names?

MS: Giving a name is a way of ascribing cultural value and representation. Growing up in the UK, I didn't see many strongly African designs out there that I could pull from, so I take a lot of inspiration from my language and my culture. The Okuta collection is inspired by 14th-century Yoruba stone murals; its name mirrors the solid, robust and bold nature of stone as a material.

NBO: Do you have a favorite material to work with?

MS: I've worked with a wide range of timber—oak, zebrano, ash, mahogany and maple. It's a warm and malleable material that can be manipulated in so many different ways. Timber reminds me of home—of Nigeria and of my grandma, who used to make wooden toys for us when we were younger.

NBO: How do you create an aesthetic that's influenced by, but not tied to, African arts and crafts?

MS: In the beginning, a lot of people didn't really understand my work—it wasn't African enough, nor sufficiently European. My work showcases a different side of African design, beyond the caricatured colors and motifs. I'm not trying to create a statement or to enforce a new wave of African design: My work is about me, who I am and how I see the world. I absorb what's around me.

NBO: Is it always about what you see?

MS: Sound plays a role in my work through music, which I love. Whenever I'm designing, I think about how the sound that I'm playing is going to interact with that object. When we were casting the Nrin vessels, for example, I was listening to Miles Davis' *Time After Time* and was mesmerized by the way the sounds of jazz bounced off the metal. Sound is an interesting concept to play with.

KINFOLK

BEAUTY IN THE BEAT
How rhythm shapes our lives.

Rhythm has great significance in music and poetry beyond simply propelling the track or verse forward. And its role varies around the world: Unlike in Western music, for example, where the melody takes precedence, West African songs are generally polyrhythmic, meaning that they layer two or more conflicting rhythms to represent the fabric of life and the dialogue of human relationships.

Our actual dialogue—language—is also governed by rhythm; everything from syllable stress to pauses and pitch help to get across what we are trying to communicate to the listener. Barack Obama, for instance, regularly employs a dramatic pause to add weight and gravitas to poignant moments in his speeches, and studies have shown that a reassuring, meditative rhythm has been proven to help to reduce anxiety: Those working with nonverbal children have found that they are more likely to speak when offered a clear, drummed-out rhythm to follow.

From the first heartbeat heard through a sonogram to the moment it comes to flatline, with every slowing or quickening in between, rhythm is proof that life exists. When our circadian rhythm—the internal 24-hour clock that dictates our sleep patterns, hormones, body temperature and appetite—is disrupted, we find ourselves unable to function. Similarly, the pace of our respiration and menstrual cycles can betray our physical or emotional health. As something so innate within us, it's no surprise that rhythm is crucial to all areas of our life.

WORDS
JOHN OVANS
PHOTO
CHIRON DUONG

28

STARTERS

THE PIZZA EFFECT
A digest on food appropriation.

WORDS
PRECIOUS ADESINA
PHOTO
THOMAS ALBDORF

On a trip to Naples in the 1830s, the American inventor and painter Samuel Morse described pizza as looking "like a piece of bread that has been taken reeking out of the sewer." At the time, pizza was primarily sold by street vendors and comprised a simple base and very few toppings (often just tomato). Consequently, pizza was associated with deprivation and left out of Neapolitan cuisine when cookbooks emerged at the end of the 19th century.

Only when Italian immigrants arrived in the United States in the late 1800s did the fate of pizza change. As the dish slowly spread across America, it was tweaked by restaurateurs to appeal to a broader range of communities. Pizza evolved from a no-frills street snack to a dish with a variety of styles and toppings worthy of brick-and-mortar restaurants in every town across the nation.

Eventually, Americans visiting Italy came to expect the sort of pizza they knew and loved at home. "Italians, responding to this demand, developed pizzerias to meet American expectations," wrote Stephen Jenkins, a professor of religious studies at Humboldt State University in California, in a 2002 article. "Delighted with their discovery of 'authentic' Italian pizza, Americans subsequently developed chains of 'authentic' Italian brick-oven pizzerias [back home]. Hence, Americans met their own reflection in the other and were delighted."

Now, when any aspect of a country's culture is exported, adapted and reimported back to the original country in its newer form, it's known as "the Pizza effect"—a term coined in 1970 by the late Agehananda Bharati, a professor of anthropology at Syracuse University for over 30 years. Bharati used "the pizza effect" to explain why certain Indian philosophies and practices had gained newfound popularity in India during the mid-20th century. One of the most famous examples he drew on was yoga, once considered a spiritual or religious discipline until a watered-down version was introduced to Americans in the late 1800s. After a century of adaptation in the US, yoga has famously found a new home among health and wellness enthusiasts worldwide as a form of exercise—including in India itself.

While the influences cultures have on one another can lead to exciting inventions, there can be a sinister side too. Both yoga and pizza were not as popular or valued in their home countries until they had been Americanized. In some cases, these newer versions can become so far removed from their roots, and yet still described (and widely accepted) as "authentic," that they can actually alter the self-understanding of the origin culture.

In the book *A Postcolonial People: South Asians in Britain*, Sophia Ahmed wrote of how colonization and migration brought South Asian food to Britain, apart from one of the most popular "Indian" dishes in the UK: chicken tikka masala. "Had it not been for the British experience, there would have been no gravy [masala] with our chicken today," Ahmed wrote. "In other words, chicken tikka masala exists only because of the fusion of these cultural experiences and, as a consequence, is now eaten both in Britain and throughout South Asia."

It's inevitable that cultures influence each other for better or worse, but when adapting even the simplest recipes—like pizza—we must acknowledge and appreciate the true history of how they arrived on our plates. After all, the difference between a Neapolitan pizza and a Chicago deep-dish are invariably clear, so the history behind them should be too.[1]

---

(1) Unfortunately, however, the history of Chicago-style pizza is unclear. Most reports attribute the 1940s invention to the Malnati family, who were associated with the city's Pizzeria Uno, but precisely which member of the family came up with the original recipe is debated.

REID BARTELME & HARRIET JUNG

WORDS
ANNICK WEBER
PHOTO
VALERIE CHIANG

An inquiry into costume design.

The New York–based duo Reid Bartelme and Harriet Jung design costumes for dance productions, combining their fashion schooling with Bartelme's background as a trained dancer. In the past dozen or so years, they have designed costumes for everything from ballet to Broadway shows, but it's in contemporary dance, when working with the likes of Pam Tanowitz and Justin Peck, that the two feel most at home. Bartelme and Jung's practice is rooted in an understanding that the role of costume designers is as integral to a performance as that of the choreographer, dancer, set designer or musician. "In our research, we always come back to the great 20th-century artists, operating in this beautiful collaborative ethos," says Bartelme, referring to the Ballets Russes and Merce Cunningham's association with John Cage. "It's an endless pool of inspiration."

ANNICK WEBER: You met while studying fashion design at New York's Fashion Institute of Technology. What made you shift your focus to costume design?

REID BARTELME: There are so many ways of approaching fashion in terms of wearability and performance, but at the end of the day, garments have to sell. With costumes, we're free from the capitalist systems that fashion is built on. We can explore an entirely new avenue of aesthetic thought with each project we turn to.

HARRIET JUNG: That's what's so liberating about costume design. A choreographer can come to us with a very specific visual goal in mind, which can be restrictive, but more often leads to an interesting creative process.

AW: What makes a costume successful?

RB: The conversation between the costume and what's going on on stage is key. It's important not only that the clothes are functional, but also functioning artistically with the space, the dancers, the music and lighting. No matter how beautiful a fabric or fitting, if there's a proportion issue, it's difficult to see past it.

AW: How do you find a balance between infusing the costumes with a design traceable to your studio and interpreting the choreographer's vision?

HJ: There's this push and pull during the design development, which doesn't exist in fashion. If a creative director says no, it's a no; whereas we're in dialogue with a choreographer. There might be certain design elements that we're willing to let go, but we'll push for others to stay. Sometimes seeing a design on a body is all it takes to understand why certain aspects [of the costume] will benefit the work. It's important to put things on a stage.

AW: Does your background as a trained dancer come in handy at this stage, Reid?

RB: It allows me to bring a lot of experiential information into the design process. Harriet is up to speed on what's needed in terms of fabrics and pattern-making techniques and actually, it has been very useful working with someone who doesn't come from dance, who asks, "Why does this not work? Why are we not trying this?"

AW: Which one of your costumes would you say has been particularly boundary-pushing?

HJ: We designed these red costumes for Pam Tanowitz's *Gustave Le Gray*, which had strips of fabric hanging from the dancers' arms and neck down to their ankles. Generally, choreographers are afraid of anything that might hinder the dancers' movement, but Pam let us push forward with the design because we felt the visual elements worked so well together. We thought, "If the dancers get caught, they'll get uncaught." And sometimes they did, and it was okay. It became part of the performance.

RB: It's always this tension between the body and the garment itself that generates a lot of beautiful things.

KINFOLK

32

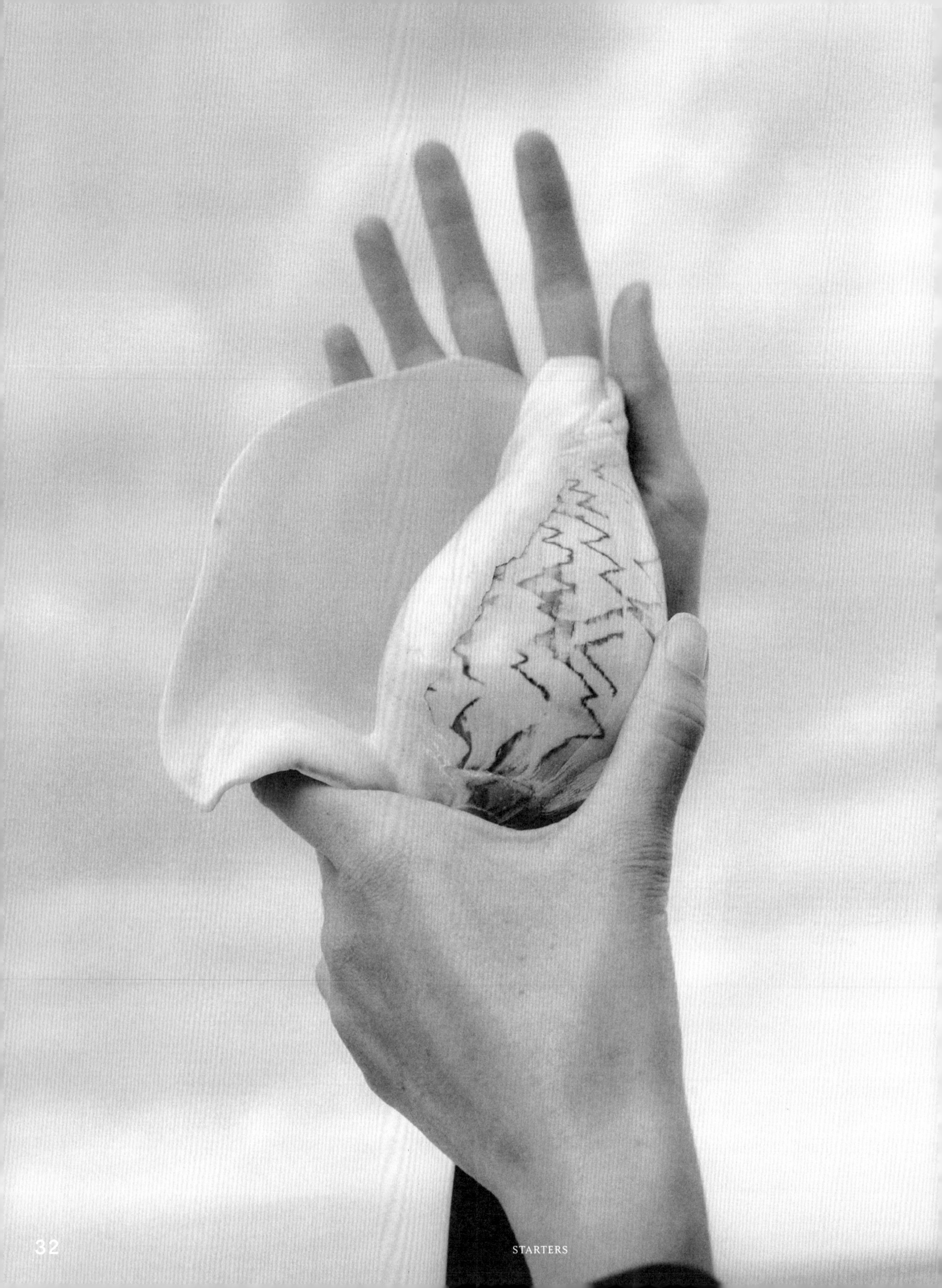

STARTERS

BETWEEN THE EARS
A guide to the lost art of listening.

WORDS
ALICE VINCENT
PHOTO
KELLY GEDDES

Last year, I bought some new headphones. Clever, sleek little white things that announced themselves with a reassuring chirrup. They transported me into a new wireless realm of sound after years of living without a means of listening to music—or anything, really—while on the move. In London, where I live, I pass hundreds of strangers every day and nearly all of them are plugged into something. Now I am among them.

It has never been easier to listen, and it has never been more difficult. We can have a friend on the phone while interacting with a salesclerk (although the etiquette on this remains dubious), and we have access to thousands of songs with a flick of the finger. We can find great speeches and inspiring performances from decades ago on YouTube, and hear the minutiae of our loved ones' lives in a voice note pinged across the ether. But while access is easy, focus is more challenging.

Listening is a skill and one that has always been hampered by modern life, regardless of when that modernity arrived. Even the Stoics were aware of it as something to be mastered: "We have two ears and one mouth so that we can listen twice as much as we speak," advised Epictetus, the ancient Greek philosopher. Two millennia later we're still struggling: In the past few years alone there has been a flurry of books dedicated to the art of listening—from journalists (*You're Not Listening* by Kate Murphy), social skills coaches (*How to Listen with Intention* by Patrick King) and even librettists (*How to Listen* by Katie Colombus). Listening today is difficult, Murphy argues, not only because modern life is noisy—all those notifications, all that auditory overstimulation—but because it enables us to curate what we want to hear.

But beyond the passive consumption of noise, we're missing out by being poor listeners in person, too. Murphy claims that our increased inability to listen to one another is a major contributor to the current global loneliness epidemic. Because for everything we can consume through our ears, the best listening happens with those things that are harder to record: the idle compliments from a kind stranger; the long, deep conversations with an old friend or a new lover; the gentle breathing of our sleeping children. These are among the everyday things that make a life but they are easily missed. Listening to them happens when we cut through the other noise, not just the readily accessed music on our devices, but also the desire to scroll through for another snippet of video to watch.

When we do listen well, though, it serves as a kind of connection. To do so means blocking the noise outside of our conversations; it also requires listening without placing ourselves in the experiences we're hearing about and without expecting a space for our own reciprocity.[1] Listening is an art because it demands the same consciousness required of any act of creation. Truly engage with what someone is saying and it can take both parties into a new place: beyond the stories we tell ourselves, and into those we share with one another.

(1) The late psychologist Carl Rogers called this skill "active listening" in a 1957 book of the same name. The listener "does not passively absorb the words which are spoken to him," Rogers wrote. "He actively tries to grasp the facts and the feelings in what he hears, and he tries, by his listening, to help the speaker work out his own problems."

LEASE ON LIFE
How to make rentals more meaningful.

In the 18th century, a peculiar genre of fiction became popular among British readers. Known as "it-narratives," these stories were told by objects—spoons, waistcoats, sedans, you name it—and were designed to show the many hands a single object passed through in the riotous early days of consumer culture. Relishing in the exchange, leasing and circulation of things, it-narratives exposed how temporary "ownership" really was.

This fluid circulation of things resonates with what, in the 21st century, has become the "sharing economy"—where people increasingly rent, rather than purchase, their items. Now more than ever, it's not just real estate that's up for hire: it's movies, vacuum cleaners, wardrobes, cameras. Want to nuzzle a cat without emptying the litter box? Or hang an artwork knowing you're moving in a month? The rental marketplace can fulfill these desires, with users on sites like Fat Llama and Peerby wheeling out items that range from the vital—cars and storage space—to the comically mundane, like popcorn makers and novelty mugs (only $7.50 a day!).[1]

The flexibility of this network is a huge plus, letting people populate their lives with new delights without requiring huge sums of money or a long-term commitment. But renting the things that make your home feel homey, or your daily life more affordable, may backfire. The objects we own are crucial in cultivating our sense of self: They're not only statements of taste and expression, they also bear imprints of personal history, rooting us amid the dysphoria of our evolving lives.

So how can we foster feelings of belonging when stuff comes and goes? The answer might lie in leaning into the transience. If objects anchor us, they can also consume us—we become "possessed by possessions," as the scholar Bill Brown puts it. A more impermanent attachment to our things resists this tendency to hoard and covet, turning our focus instead to the joy of selection. Thoughtfully choosing, rather than mindlessly accruing, removes the tyranny of stuff, leaving space to figure ourselves out through ever-renewing moments of curation. And it's with this exploration that objects—even rented ones—can feel like home again.

(1) Rentals are becoming more commonplace in the fashion industry. In the UK, platforms like Hurr (a website) and By Rotation (an app) typically ask for 10% of the retail price and have become so popular that high street retailers such as H&M are now introducing rental sections into flagships.

WORDS
ANNABEL BAI JACKSON
PHOTO
LAUREN BAMFORD

35

KINFOLK

WORDS
MARAH EAKIN
PHOTO
SEBASTIÁN FAENA

There was a time, not too long ago, when you had to make a phone call to do just about anything, from arranging dates with friends to sussing out what time a store closed. The phone's primacy went even further in the workplace, where it was an essential tool in building relationships, making sales and simply getting shit done.

That's all changed, of course. These days, you can pop into an office and not see a single desk phone. More and more people eschew phone calls for lengthy emails, cringing at the prospect of yet another worthless Zoom catch-up. The art of the phone call is being lost, and it's a tragedy.

Workplace communication expert Amy Gallo advises that a well-placed phone call can not only speed along a project, but help stave off interoffice conflict. "With an email, you don't have context," she explains. "I don't know what your facial expression was, I don't know if you're sending it from a hospital waiting room because your kid is sick. If you pick up the phone, I get a sense of what's going on from context clues and that encourages natural empathy."

Getting on a call can also help skirt the online disinhibition trap, whereby you might use a tone that's spicier or brusquer than you'd opt for IRL. If a project or a conversation is already going a little awry, a quick call can help clear the air and build connection—especially if you're in a remote work environment. "One of the best mindsets you can have for conflict resolution is this idea that you're in it together," says Gallo. "Hearing someone's voice on a phone call encourages collaboration, resolution and a path forward."

Are you loathe to chat—or anxious about how to nudge a colleague to answer the phone? Gallo recommends acknowledging that openly by saying, "I know no one likes to talk on the phone these days, but I think it'll be a little quicker to just chat for five minutes and hammer this out," or, "I'm having trouble explaining myself on email. Would you mind talking?" It might seem awkward at first, but with practice and perseverance, even the most phone-averse can learn to love a dial tone again.

—

TOUGH CALL
A simple tool for workplace conflicts.

MINOR LAPSES
The new way of doing nothing.

WORDS
ASHER ROSS
PHOTO
ANDONI BERISTAIN

Most people find it hard to do nothing. Which is not to say we have trouble finding idle distractions. We're quite good at that. Scroll through our feeds? Sure. Hang around the house with a friend? Easy. But the idea of doing truly *nothing* seems impossible. Sitting alone, motionless, with no distraction. It's nearly distressing.

Unless you're Dutch. In that case, you may know all about *niksen*—the act of doing nothing at all. The word transliterates roughly as "nothing-doing," and in practice, means actively deciding to sit and surrender the rudder of your mind. It should not be confused with meditation, which is a disciplined journey into the self. The point of niksen is to forgo mental discipline altogether. To give the mind a stretch.

If you've ever been exhausted by a project, fallen into a daydream and then come out with a fresh insight, you've experienced the benefits of the practice. One way to understand how this happens is through the lens of psychoanalytic theory. To Freud and his descendants, our conscious mind—the part that can decide to do something and focus on it—sits on top of a vast unconscious that is constantly working. The unconscious can be a pest, causing us to feel sad or distracted without knowing why, but it can also be a magnificent artist. Dreams are the result of the unconscious doing its work unfettered as we sleep.

Freud thought these same dynamics pertained to daydreaming as well. He noticed that two kinds of people—children and creative writers—were able to daydream quite freely, whereas for most adults the habit becomes constrained and censored. As we age, we come to rely too heavily on our conscious minds, forcing our thoughts this way and that, forgetting what our unconscious can do when we allow it to play. Or as Freud wrote of children (and writers): "Might we not say that every child at play behaves like a creative writer, in that he creates a world of his own, or rather, rearranges the things of his world in a new way which pleases him?"

Since it came into vogue outside the Netherlands, niksen has attracted interest as a possible salve for workplace burnout. No doubt the findings will be good. But to enter into niksen expecting a timely benefit is like watching a pot of water boil. The first sign of niksen isn't a eureka moment, but pleasure. Yes, problem-solving flourishes when we cease to bully our attention spans. But the process itself is the reward. To paraphrase the ancient Roman orator Cicero, who was no slouch when it came to productivity: "He does not seem to me to be a free man who does not sometimes do nothing."

—

PITCH PERFECT
In praise of darkness.

Ever since the world first formed, night has followed day. It is a certainty hardwired into living things. Plants will boost their scent or close up based on the time of day. Animals will hunt or mate, give birth or hatch, at a particular moment relative to dawn or dusk. "This biological clock, the circadian rhythm is ancient, shared and completely fundamental," ecologist Johan Eklöf writes in *The Darkness Manifesto*.

It is also under threat. "Light pollution"—a term first coined by astronomers searching for ever more remote places to study the night sky—has come to be used by ecologists, physiologists and neurologists who study the effects of disappearing night. Eklöf gives the example of the dramatic decline in insect populations over the past 30 years, one of the biggest impacts of light pollution. Anyone who has seen a moth trapped in a beam of light knows how insects can be easily confused by artificial light, where they exhaust themselves and become vulnerable to predators. As half of all insects are nocturnal, and with the vast majority of plants depending on insects for pollination, this in itself could prove catastrophic for our fragile ecosystem.

Yet light pollution has also been found to affect everything from the immune systems of urban birds (increasing the risk of viruses spreading to humans) to the reproductive cycles of coral reefs. Humans might lack the special adaptations of nocturnal animals but we are no less dependent on darkness. Melatonin, the hormone that tells the body to go to sleep, is only released when the eyes begin to stop perceiving light, a process that can be inhibited by phone screens or street lights, leading to difficulties sleeping and the risk of long-term health issues including heart disease, obesity and depression. Eklöf makes a case for the urgent need to reconcile society's need for light with nature's need for darkness, but also laments how estranged we have become from the dark. "Few people know real darkness or what a starry sky looks like," he writes. Eklöf goes on to note Jun'ichiro Tanizaki's observation in *In Praise of Shadows*, a seminal essay on Japanese aesthetics, that meaning in art, architecture and literature is not found in light but in varying degrees of darkness. In many ways, you could say the same for life on Earth.

WORDS
GEORGE UPTON
PHOTO
MAYA BEANO

MARCIO KOGAN

WORDS
MANJU SARA RAJAN
PHOTOS
RAPHAEL LUCENA

On the pursuit of perfection.

Behind Marcio Kogan in his São Paulo office sits a kaleidoscope of objects—memorial trinkets from his adventures in filmmaking and architecture. It's a varied collection that hints at the life of the founder of the architecture practice Studio MK27: a Hollywood star signed with his name, a movie clapboard, a *Scream* mask, a Minion toy. "Everything here has a story," he says.

Kogan began his career as a filmmaker, giving up the camera after a disastrous turn at making a feature film. Here, he explains how his love for cinema still impacts everything his award-winning firm touches—a span of work that stretches from breezy, modernist homes in Brazil to real estate projects in Dubai and plans for the Brazil Pavilion at the World Expo in Osaka in 2025.

MANJU SARA RAJAN: What made you choose architecture over films?

MARCIO KOGAN: During my architecture school years, I was simultaneously directing short films. After I graduated, I had a small office with five or six people, and I decided to direct a feature film. This was in 1988. At that point, I had a winning career in short films and awards from around the world, but the feature film was a disaster. In the end, I lost my architectural office, I lost my money, I lost everything. I loved the experience, even though it was a bit traumatic. So, I decided to be an architect full-time.

MSR: How has the experience with filmmaking impacted your architectural design practice?

MK: Directing films taught me different approaches that I brought to my architectural practice, like a special way of working where everyone participates in the process. In movies, there is also a lot of emphasis on lighting. Another thing is the way we design: My process is to create an architectural script, like a movie script. I create a story, and I imagine a character and how they would use the space. The last thing is that my buildings have a wide-screen proportion that I used to love with movies.

MSR: When I look at the props behind you in your office and watch some of the films on your projects, there's a sense of humor—an unexpected trait in architecture.

MK: I began my filmmaking career thinking about Ingmar Bergman; he was my idol. My first short film was black and white and very intellectual, and at the same time it was ridiculous. All the actors were inexperienced, and how would it be if Bergman shot a film with a bunch of kids?! After that, everything in my life has humor. But one day, I was conducting a class at the University of São Paulo with more than 1,000 people in the audience, and a student asked me, "Why is there no humor in your work?" I took three minutes thinking about the answer and my conclusion was that there's no humor in architecture. Can you imagine? I stood in front of so many people thinking and thinking, and the answer was that there is no humor in it!

MSR: Is it because architects take themselves so seriously?

MK: Yeah, it's not good. When I was a student, maybe some of

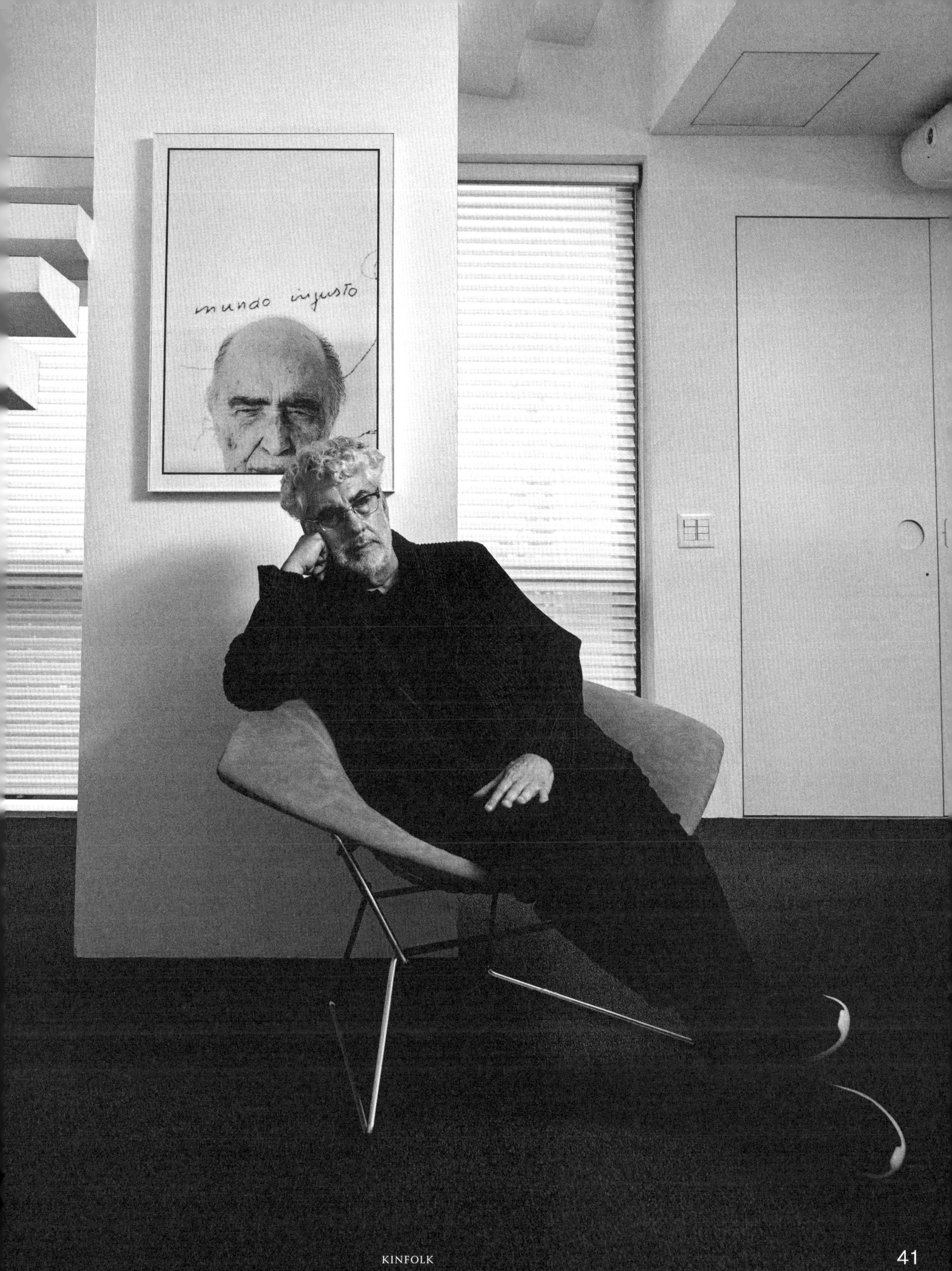
mundo injusto

STARTERS

my projects had a sense of humor, but those were theoretical.

MSR: You've worked in many topographies and cultures. How does Studio MK27 contend with multiculturalism?

MK: Everywhere that we design, we try to get a local architect and the client to bring in a little bit of their feeling of the place. For example, when we worked on a project in India, we had an intensive course on *vastu* [a traditional Indian system of architecture]. They told me that vastu is very important when it comes to real estate, so I studied it beforehand and we had a person working in the client's office in Delhi. In the end, it's a mix of our culture and theirs, and that's what the clients are looking for.

MSR: How does a large firm like Studio MK27—which is named for the 27 people in the practice—work on a unified philosophy?

MK: It's not easy because I'm obsessed with perfection. It is difficult to be so exacting when you have 50 architects. So, we're 27 now. When I was producing my feature film and needed to be out of the office for six months, it was a disaster. Now, there are more than 10 architects who've been working with me for 15 to 20 years. This makes a big difference, because quality improves with a mature team.

MSR: What does luxury mean for you and does it influence your design philosophy?

MK: I think it's everything, taken together—an entire lifestyle. I don't believe in the kind of luxury that's gold and chandeliers. We stand for the opposite of that. We relate to elegance, simplicity. This is the idea we sell. It's not so easy to find nowadays. It was there during the Mies van der Rohe years; Oscar Niemeyer was an elegant guy. But now, the idea is innovation at any cost.

MSJ: Perhaps it has to do with the internet—drama catches attention.

MK: I've learned that we have our own audience, and that we don't have so many competitors in this area where there's no drama. For instance, in Dubai, a client called us and said, "Bring your houses to our project," so we're designing nine buildings—a new kind of real estate project for a client who said he wants luxury apartments that are not in a tall building. It will be seven floors or so—something special for people who understand our way of thinking, and something different in Dubai.

MSR: How do you create your signature blend of architecture, interior design and landscape design?

MK: My father was an important architect here in São Paulo who died young, when he was just 36 years old. And I lived in a house where he designed everything, with very good taste. It was a house with a lot of technology, but of course it was the technology of the 1950s—a moment when architects were trying to break barriers and bring technology into houses. He designed everything, even the art. I think that was an influence for me. Some years ago, we decided that we must design interiors because we know best how a space must behave and how to transmit the intention of the design correctly. We'd had bad experiences where we finish an incredible project, and then the interior design destroys it. By doing the interior design, we've been able to create a language and it's now an important part of our practice. We also have incredible collaborators for landscape design, so there's a strong relationship between indoors and outdoors: You don't know where the home stops. To achieve that near-perfection, everything has to be important at the same level: the architecture, the interior and the landscape design. Maybe you'll never have 10 out of 10, but this is our way of following a path to perfection.

GOOD ENOUGH
The case for plainness.

It's a mistake to believe that the primary goal of design is beauty. Aesthetic satisfaction is, and should be, a byproduct. MUJI, the successful Japanese product design company, has confidently accepted this idea: Rather than relying on visual enticements to capture customers' attention, MUJI produces what it calls "quality goods" that it feels are better characterized by terms like "simplicity" and "emptiness" than by "beauty." The company's three-word motto, "This will do," underlies its approach to aesthetic considerations. It is up to the consumer, says MUJI, to fill its products with their own feelings.[1]

This reasonable stance toward product design might seem unusual in a discipline so committed to the visual, but it isn't new. The early modern Austrian architect Adolf Loos sardonically criticized men's fashion in 1898, mocking a widespread "craving for beauty": "The Medici Venus, the Pantheon, a picture by Botticelli, a song by Burns—of course these are beautiful! But a pair of trousers?" Well-dressed people, Loos argued, "abjure claims to *beauty*." Instead, they seek out good materials, excellent construction and visual reserve. In the turn-of-the-century design production Loos witnessed and critiqued, two trends were competing to replace the eclectic historical tastes of 1800s Europe—a flamboyant art nouveau and a far more austere modernism.

Modernism prevailed through the first tumultuous decades of the 20th century, coming to dominate industrial and architectural design. By then, another three-word motto, attributed to German architect Ludwig Mies van der Rohe, was beginning to take hold of designers' imaginations: "Less is more."

In spite of his own rhetoric, Mies never fully relinquished the urge to aestheticize design. His exquisitely sparse houses, for example, had chromed steel columns and walls clad with precisely book-matched marble veneers. It was British New Brutalist architects, such as Alison and Peter Smithson, who took the challenge more seriously. The Smithsons were perhaps the first modernists to overtly abjure claims to beauty, instructing builders of a 1950s house they designed to "aim at a high standard of basic construction, as in a small warehouse."

According to Rayner Banham, an early historian of Brutalism, the Smithsons' goal was to show plainly what a building "is made of, and how it works"—and no more. Their architecture was meant to be "good enough"; people could work out their own aesthetic and emotional attachments to it. This wasn't mere practicality, but unembellished truth-telling through design. The problem with Brutalism, however, was that people's reactions to it were not always (or even usually) favorable.

Consumer product design employs a more convivial palette, so a good-enough design strategy works better in that arena. When Dieter Rams, the longtime head of design at Braun, took on this challenge in the late 20th century, his motto was "As little design as possible." His intention was, he explains, to "return to simplicity" and to combat the "ruthless exploitation of people's weakness for visual and haptic signals." So, he "tended to steer well clear from this discussion about beauty and argued instead for a design that is as reduced, clear and user-oriented as possible." This is the same attitude MUJI took on 40 years ago and continues still. Enough, it seems, is enough.

WORDS
ALEX ANDERSON
PHOTO
CHRISTIAN MØLLER ANDERSEN

(1) MUJI's longtime art director Kenya Hara expands on these ideas in his book *White*. "The role of design is not to surprise or draw people's attention in with novelty," he writes. "It is to give humanity a chance to notice the wisdom accumulated over the ages that is hidden in all sorts of things."

45

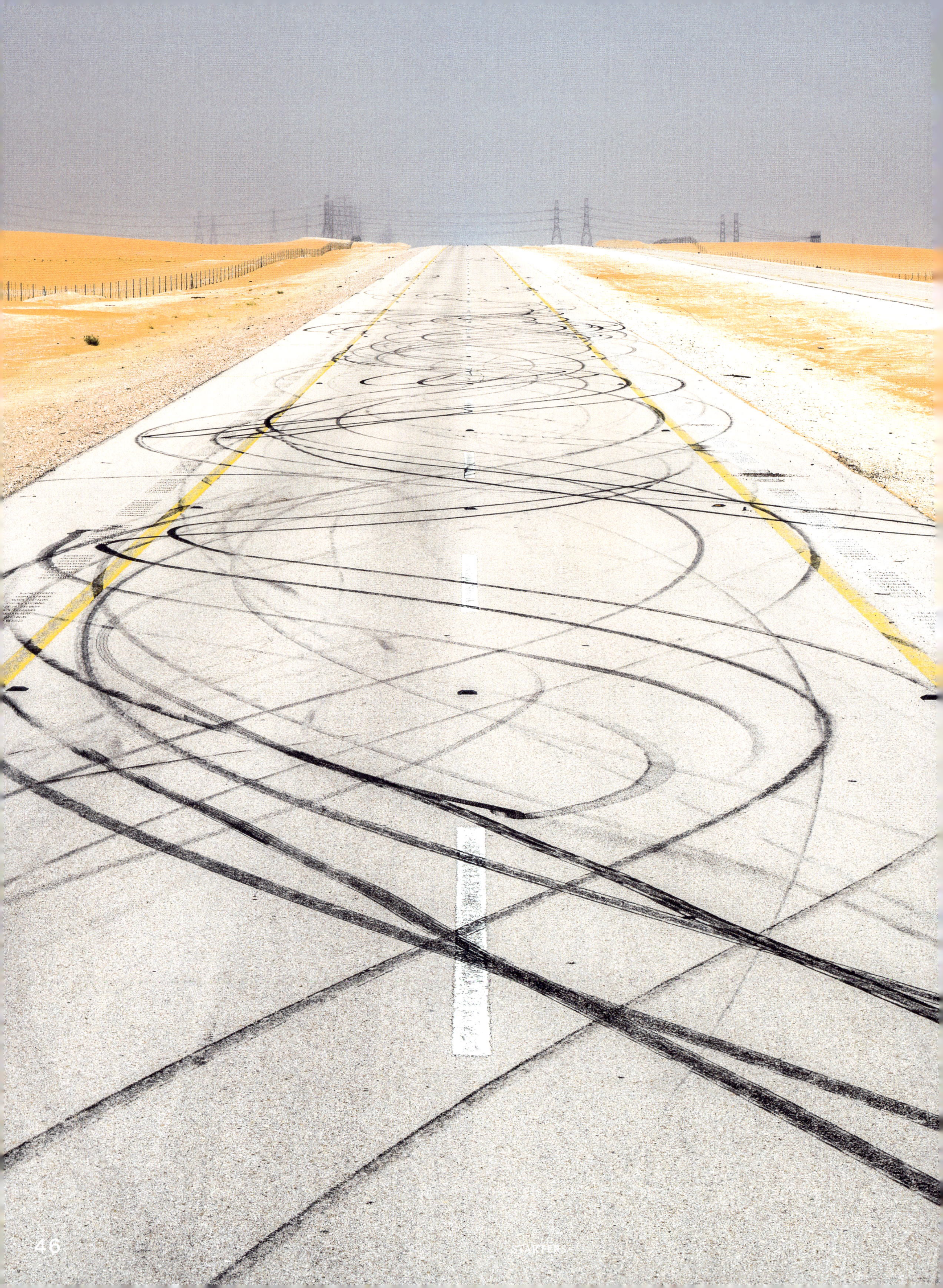

NELL WULFHART

WORDS
JENNA MAHALE
PHOTO
PETER BOGACZEWICZ

Advice from a decision coach.

People are always coming to Nell Wulfhart with questions: Should I break up? Should I have a baby? Should I take this job? Should I adopt a dog? Should I give the dog back? "That was a couple of people, actually," she says, speaking from her home in Montevideo, Uruguay.

Wulfhart, a decision coach who previously wrote a travel column for *The New York Times*, left her native Philadelphia to live abroad more than two decades ago. In 2013, friends convinced her to make a business out of her knack for guiding others. Now, Wulfhart has built a successful career on the strength of a simple but powerful idea: that most seemingly indecisive people are simply looking for a permission slip to do what they really want.

JENNA MAHALE: How would you describe what you do?
NELL WULFHART: I help people make big decisions. In fact, I kind of make them for them. Somewhere inside themselves, most people know what they want to do, but they don't *know* that they know it. So, I figure out what that is, and tell them that it's okay to do it.
JM: What are the most important things to consider when it comes to making a life decision?
NW: I usually ask people to do two exercises before our sessions. First, make a list of their values: the things that make them happy in everyday life. For me, that's never setting an alarm clock in the morning, being able to wear a tracksuit around the house and not having to go out if I don't feel like it. I also ask them to try and envision their lives in the future—one year from now, five years from now, 10 years from now. Just a sketch of what their ideal life might look like. People really struggle with that one. I understand . . . I struggle with it too. But I've found it to be really helpful when it comes to making big decisions, because what you want can become immediately obvious. Like, "Oh, five years from now, I want to have a kid. So maybe I shouldn't take this three-year secondment in Dubai."
JM: How would you advise someone who's having trouble moving on in their life?
NW: Whether it's about a relationship or a job, it's important to remember that some regret is unavoidable with any major decision. It might seem difficult to pick up and move somewhere else, but it's really not. It just requires a plane ticket and a little research about visas, and it can be so worth it. And if you don't like it, you can always go back. Though people might think that's depressing, I think it's kind of liberating. It makes it easier to make one of those choices, because there is no perfect decision. I mean, there are good decisions, but we can only control the decision. We can't control the outcome.
JM: Do you often feel like a therapist, or do you ever see it that way?
NW: I'm not a therapist. I'm not a behavioral scientist. I'm just somebody who's really good at making decisions. People do tell me very deep personal things, and it involves a lot of active listening, so it can feel a little like therapy sometimes. But I think therapy tends to focus on the why: *Why do I feel this way? Why am I stuck?* For me, the why is almost always irrelevant. My job is to get people unstuck and moving. What decision is going to make your life better now and in the future? Let's get you doing that.

WORDS
SUYIN HAYNES
PHOTO
GEORGE BYRNE

Politely declining an invitation can be a tricky tightrope to walk. It's fair to assume that most invites are extended with good intentions and sincerity, but sometimes seeing them pop up across a plethora of digital platforms can evoke an involuntary shudder.

On the one hand, there are plenty of reasons why you *should* grab that coffee, why you *should* go to that party, why you *should* do that task. But on the other, it's perfectly fine to simply not *want* to do any of these things. You don't need to have an elaborate reason or another obligation to fulfill—just not feeling inclined is enough.

It may sound a little cantankerous, but there is truth to the idea of recharging our social batteries—a phrase that seems to have seeped into popular vernacular lately. A 2020 study from the University of Finland (where there's a well-known culture of avoiding small talk) showed that sociable behavior resulted in later fatigue and tiredness from participants. The researchers suggested that being around others required more exertion compared to being in solitude.

The delicacy of the dilemma really lies in how to communicate the "no." But delivering a response with a balance of care and honesty is usually the best way to go: Opening with a thank-you is a given. What follows depends on both the content of the invite, and your relationship with the person extending it. Instead of a flat-out rejection, one brief line of context can be helpful. If it's not a good time for you to take on another project, or if you're feeling too low in energy to attend a big event, then share those feelings. In giving a generous response, you'll hopefully receive a generous reception. Be cautious of going overboard though—lengthy and elaborate responses can risk sounding like you're protesting a little *too* much—and forego jargon like "bandwidth," aiming instead for straightforward honesty in your words.

Remember that it's the invitation you're declining—not the person. Use this to guide the language of your reply with grace. The more you practice, the less awkward it becomes.

HOW TO SAY NO
And why you might want to.

Part 2.
FEATURES
An actor, a chef, four artists & a dancer.
50 — 112

50	Mamoudou Athie
60	Hanging Out with Andy Baraghani
66	Studio Visit: Heidi Gustafson
74	Jenny Odell
92	Mass Destruction
96	Dancing with Ryan Heffington
104	A World of Difference

Photography
LUKE LOVELL

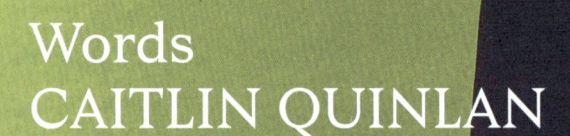

Words
CAITLIN QUINLAN

Mamoudou ATHIE:

THE SHAPE-SHIFTING ACTOR IS ON A ROLL.

Styling
CARLEE WALLACE

(above)　Athie wears a sweater by COURRÈGES from Nordstrom.
(P. 48)　He wears an outfit by OUR LEGACY and shoes by BEPOSITIVE from Nordstrom.
(P. 49)　He wears a cardigan by KENZO and trousers by LUCA FALONI.

From the Greek Weird Wave cinema of Yorgos Lanthimos to all-out Pixar whimsy, actor Mamoudou Athie is taking show business in his stride. He tells *Caitlin Quinlan* why community theater might be next.

Mamoudou Athie exudes such warmth that when we begin talking in the lush courtyard of the Carlton Cannes Hotel one afternoon in May, it feels like we've known each other forever. The actor—who is in town to attend the Cannes Film Festival's closing night premiere of his new Pixar film, *Elemental*—is thrilled to talk about acting as a craft and is meticulously detailed about his process. "Now we're gonna get into the weeds!" he says with a laugh. Throughout our conversation, he refills our water glasses and engages with passersby, an air of effortless relaxation in every kind gesture.

Nothing feels labored with Athie, 34, and certainly not his performances. That's not to say he hasn't worked extremely hard: The Mauritanian-born actor studied at New York's William Esper Studio before getting an MFA from the Yale School of Drama in 2014. And while it was easy for him to say he wanted to be an actor when he was a child, because it seemed like "a fun way to make some money," he soon realized the business wasn't that simple—nor was that what acting truly meant to him. Athie's array of work across theater, film—blockbusters, animation, independent cinema—and television is a testament to the dynamism he's developed as an actor, but it also hints at his desire for liberation in his work.

"Studying gave me technique and a way to work—a real system," he says, with the soft gravitas of a seasoned theater actor in his voice. "It gave me a lot of ways to inhabit different kinds of characters and a lot of faith in myself to inhabit different worlds." These tools have allowed him to deftly switch between the absurd comedy of FX miniseries *Oh Jerome, No*; the familial drama *Uncorked*, in which he played an aspiring sommelier ("that role was the reason I got *Elemental*," he says); and *The Get Down*, a Baz Luhrmann Netflix extravaganza about the New York rap scene in the 1970s in which he played musical pioneer Grandmaster Flash.

He's not concerned with being "of the moment," as he puts it. "I recognize through this acting process what I want overall in my life is freedom," he continues. "That's why I'm an actor—obviously, there are some restrictions, as in any job, but if it's all working out then there's a lot of freedom that is afforded to you." Besides, going from a blockbuster like *Jurassic World: Dominion* to the independent, art house environment of *AND*—Greek Weird Wave director Yorgos Lanthimos' forthcoming movie—is "all the same" to Athie. "Someone calls 'action' and then we do the scene. Sure, it might be magnified depending on the project, but when it comes down to it, it's just like talking to another person. My first job was with Baz Luhrmann and I was playing Grandmaster Flash—nothing will be scarier than that. Anytime I'm scared I'm like, *Hold on, you did that on your first big job? Yeah, everything's fine.*"

Athie has fond memories of almost everything he's worked on since, perhaps in part due to a kind of mantra he has applied to his career choices—"I only want to work with people that want to work with me"—and the questions he asks of the roles he plays: "What do they like and dislike? And what is good for him and bad for him?" The overarching narrative that their answers may imply about a character's path in life makes up the bulk of his system and practice. But he also believes that it's essential to look beyond the confines of the script or the moment in the character's life that the film might capture. "When you have a character's super objective, everything is clear to you. You can do more detailed work on the scene and you don't have to worry about how you're going to say this or that because the character just drapes over it all," he explains. Through his work, he simply knows "who the person that I'm playing really is from top to bottom."

In *Elemental*—an allegory about cultural diversity and disparate elements finding a home together—Athie plays Wade Ripple, an easygoing if sensitive water element who falls in love with hot-tempered fire element Ember (Leah Lewis). In this world, fire elements are a minority community and Ember's immigrant parents, who left their home behind to find a better life for their daughter, expect her to find a fire partner and take over the family business. For Athie, who moved to the United States at six months old when his diplomat father sought political asylum, the story resonated deeply.[1] "I'm an immigrant. I became a permanent citizen of the United States while making the film and there's so many things that paralleled my life in terms of familial sacrifice," he says. "My dad came to the States doing all kinds of jobs. The man had two master's degrees and he put all of that aside for the sake of his family. I can't imagine that level of sacrifice." Athie is visibly moved as he speaks about his father; there is the sense that he could talk about his father for hours. He pulls out his phone and reads aloud a text message that his dad sent on the eve of his Cannes trip. "Hello, son," it reads, "do not be surprised, *Elemental* will win a prize. Go always with good expectations." A charming end to the festival, the film was warmly received and garnered a five-minute standing ovation.

(above)   Athie wears a turtleneck by LUCA FALONI and a jacket by HOMME PLISSÉ ISSEY MIYAKE from Nordstrom.
(opposite)   He wears a cardigan by JOHN ELLIOTT from Nordstrom.

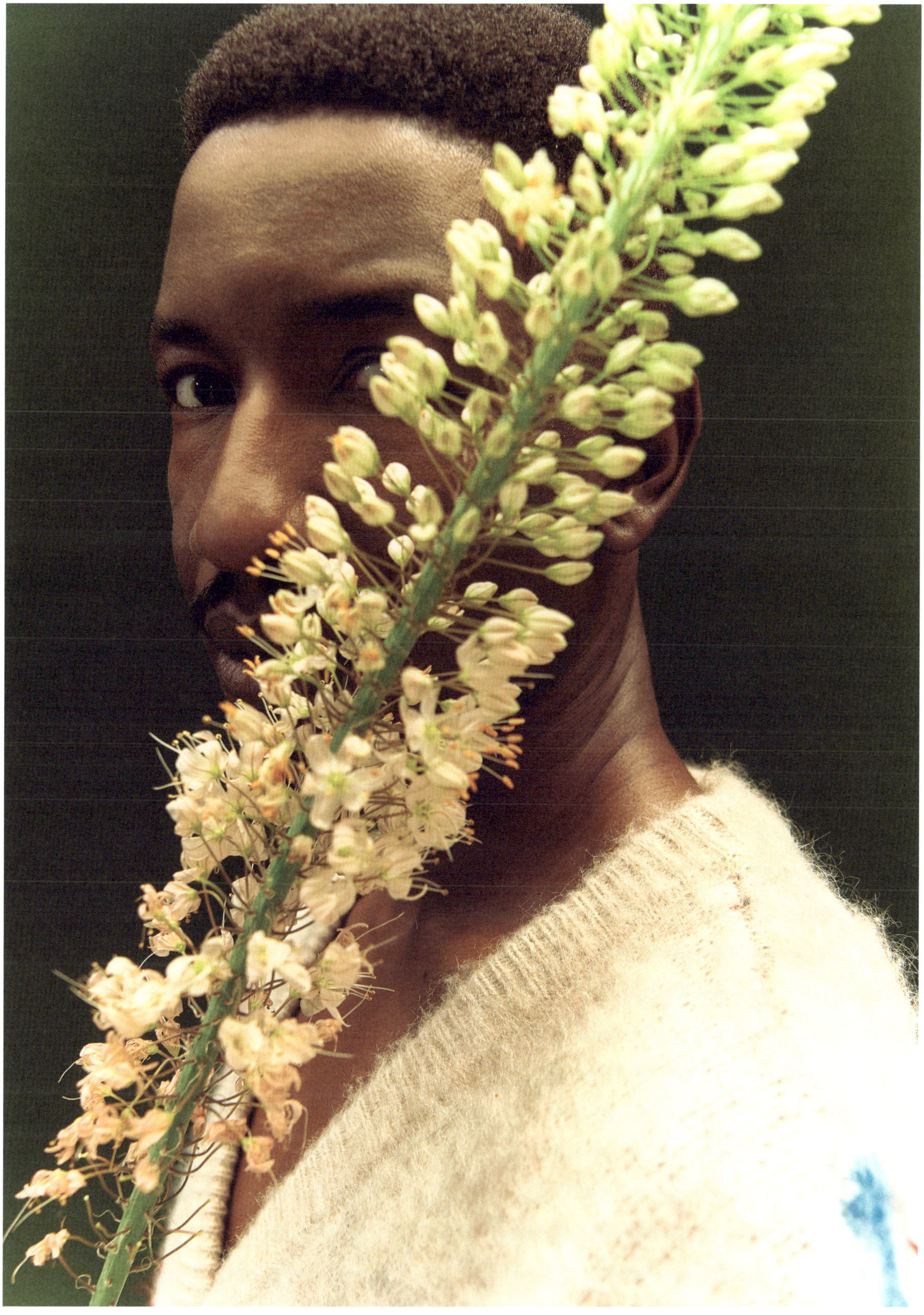

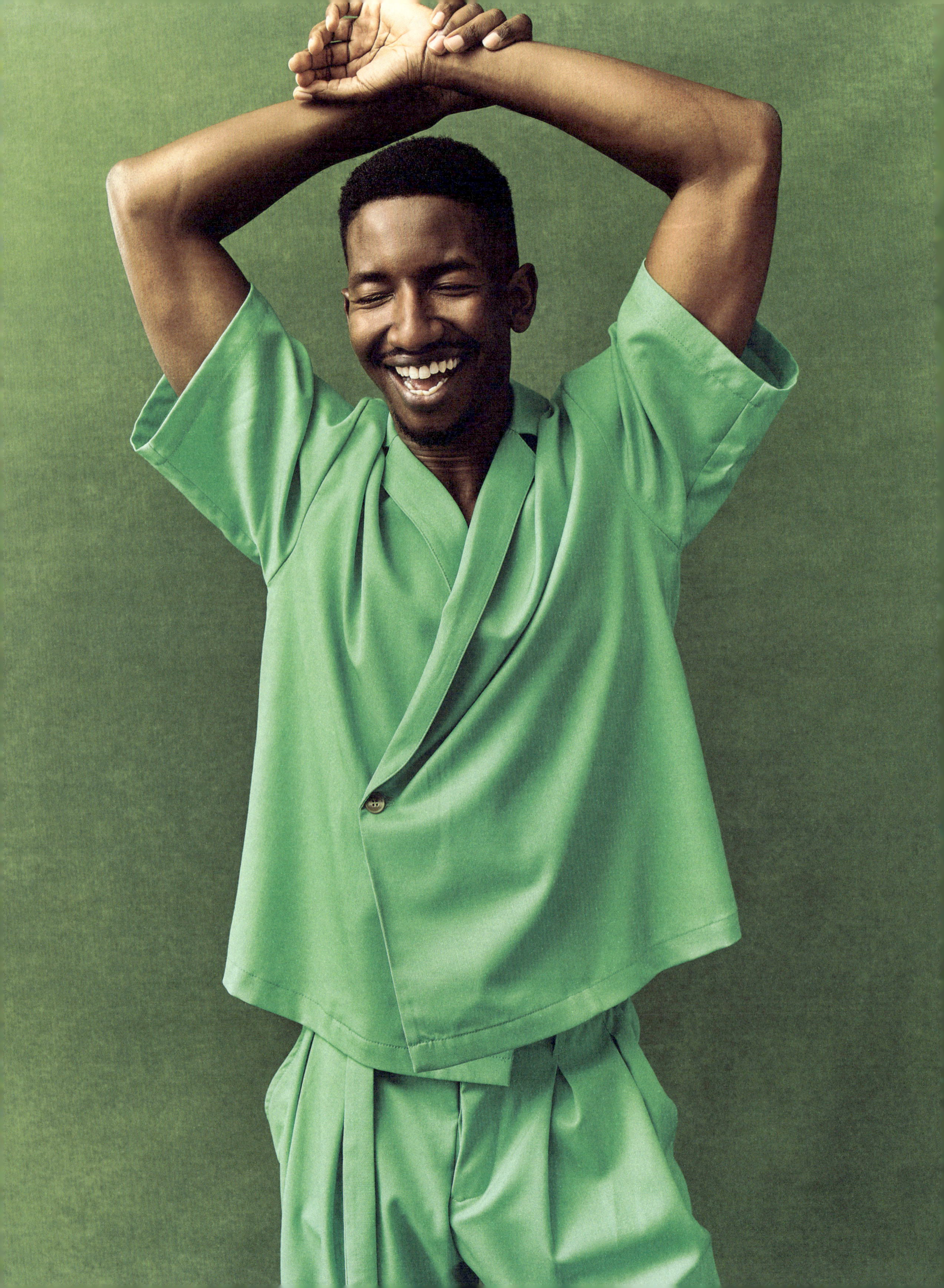

(all)   Athie wears outfits by KING & TUCKFIELD.

58

Making work that can have such an impact on people is crucial for Athie. He remembers a woman speaking to him about a play he was in during his time at Yale and, in hearing what it had meant to her, he realized, "I could do this until I'm 80." "If I could just find projects like that—that mean something to me, that can potentially touch somebody like it touched this lady—then there's some utility, and I'm not just getting away with having a cushy job like acting," he says, laughing. "That's been my guiding light for the bulk of my career." He explains that he wants his acting to be guided by emotion, and grounded in the freedom of feelings and intuition. "There are so many actors who do a wonderful job of being precise and that's fine; I can enjoy those performances when they're expertly done. But I think there's something so moving about seeing someone just let go," he says. He cites the work of Joaquin Phoenix in Spike Jonze's *Her* as "a beautiful example of somebody not thinking about how they're going to say something."

It's a skill he wants to hone further in his aspirations for the future, which are as varied as his catalog so far and include playing Hamlet, developing a project on the '80s Black punk rock scene with his friend Tunde Adebimpe, the lead singer of TV on the Radio, and returning to community theater. "My friend, the actor Yahya Abdul-Mateen II, and I have been asking ourselves lately, *What if we really risk it all?*" he says. "We've just been discussing a lot about this kind of openness and what happens if you finally get to that point. That's been the goal for me. It's been very challenging, especially when you have directors that don't necessarily work that way or aren't used to it, but I've been fortunate that anyone who's hired me wants to work with me and believes in what I've been trying to accomplish. I'm still not there, but I'm getting there, I'm getting close. It's so exciting."

(1) In April 1989, violence broke out between Arab-Berber and Black African communities in Mauritania. Known as "the 1989 events," the crisis led to the deportation of Black African citizens to Senegal and Mali, state-sponsored killings, and the purge of tens of thousands of Black Africans from the Mauritanian military and government.

"There's something so moving about seeing someone just let go."

(far left) Athie wears a sweater by ISABEL MARANT, trousers by PAS UNE MARQUE and a bracelet by PYRRHA.
(opposite) He wears a sweater by ISABEL MARANT and trousers by ADVISORY BOARD CRYSTALS.

Hanging out *with* ANDY BARAGHANI

Words ANGELA HUI

Out of the kitchen, and onto your plates, shelves and screens.

Photos EMMA TRIM

Andy Baraghani worked his way from restaurant kitchens to test kitchens. Now he's in control and cooking for himself.

"I'm sorry for all the commotion and dog barking noises, it's a bit chaotic today," says Andy Baraghani, the 33-year-old chef and *New York Times* best-selling cookbook author of *The Cook You Want to Be*, looking off into the distance, distracted. I'm on Zoom nine hours ahead from a hotel room in Frankfurt. On the other side of the Atlantic, in the Bay Area, Baraghani has just woken up and is currently spending some rare downtime at his parents' house. He's wearing a simple gray T-shirt that shows off his biceps and sipping a cup of coffee on the garden terrace. It's 9:00 a.m., and golden rays start to peek through the lush, leafy trees, lighting his face. "I mean, it's a Monday morning and there's already like 10 people here. We're planning a big dinner later," he says.

Entertaining, hosting and feeding people is very much in Baraghani's blood, and very much part of Persian culture. (His parents emigrated from Iran to Berkeley, California, in 1977, shortly before the Iranian revolution.) A family occasion involves siblings, aunties, uncles, extended family and friends cooking elaborate meals together for hours, staying up late, telling each other stories and reminiscing about childhood memories. On tonight's menu: tahchin-e esfenaj, a crispy baked saffron rice dish flecked with spinach and dried powdered lime. "My family are very supportive, and I don't think I could've written my book without them," he says. "They've hidden a copy in every room, which is a little ridiculous—I have to put it away."

Baraghani says that he didn't fully acknowledge that he was the child of immigrants until he became an adult; how it had a huge impact on how he thinks about food, how he interacts with people, and how he carries himself. But his fascination with food started here, with a Fisher-Price kitchen he received as a birthday gift when he turned four. By the time he finished high school, he had already worked in three restaurants, including at Alice Waters' famed Chez Panisse in Berkeley. "I worked up the courage to ask the staff if I could help out on Friday nights— who did I think I was?" he laughs. "Chez Panisse showed me that a kitchen was a place where I could belong."

In the time since then, he's been labeled a "food world favorite" and "the internet boyfriend of our dreams" thanks to his viral recipes—cauliflower Bolognese, tahini ranch dressing and ramen noodles with miso pesto—and the videos of him cooking them. In June, Baraghani's cookbook won a James Beard Foundation Award, which, he says, caught him totally off guard. "I never allowed myself to dream that my debut book would ever be nominated. I'm just so humbled—I'm friends with the two other nominees and I really admire their work," he says.

(opposite)   Baraghani says he first learned to cook by watching family members prepare Persian classics such as kuku sabzi (an herb-filled omelet) and chelo ba tahdig (steamed rice with a golden crust).

(opposite) Baraghani's cookbook has a recipe for fermented garlic honey (12 crushed garlic cloves in 1½ cups of raw honey; stir five times over 10 days) which, he writes, is excellent drizzled over pepperoni pizza.

The idea behind *The Cook You Want to Be*, he explains, was to empower the home cook to experiment, and to make sure that it felt like he was right there in the kitchen with them: "I want to give a deeper knowledge about food and cooking that people can take away to help them with their everyday cooking; I didn't want it to be an authority or a template, but merely a guide with amounts and indicators," he says. "When you're at a restaurant, you're very much cooking someone else's food. I've also developed hundreds of my own recipes for different publications, but they're still under the template of that publication. With this cookbook, *I* really thought about how they should read or sound."

Baraghani transitioned from the restaurant business into food media after contributing to *Saveur* magazine, where he had interned while studying food studies and cultural anthropology at New York University. Here, he learned the ropes of recipe development, writing, testing and food photography until, in 2016, after a "really long and rigorous" interview process, he bagged the senior food editor role at *Bon Appétit*. While at Condé Nast, he met his partner, Keith Pollock, a former executive at *Architectural Digest*, who he lives with in New York and who, he says, makes a mean breakfast. "I fuck with a man who makes an excellent soft scrambled egg," he laughs.

Over the past year and a half, Baraghani has been freelance. It's been a nonstop roller coaster ride, he says, but, for the first time, he's felt in control of how he wants to present recipes. He's cooked at events for brands such as Beni Rugs, Reform and Nili Lotan, created lemon, sumac and thyme CBD gummies with Rose Los Angeles, taught *Today Show* viewers how to cook sticky-sweet roast chicken (which the internet had a lot to say about), appeared on *The Drew Barrymore Show* and was invited to the White House to celebrate the Persian holiday Nowruz.

He's very flattered, but never set out to be a public figure. "It's just a very happy accident that's become part of the job," he says. "At the end of the day, if people are learning something and becoming better cooks, then that's all I want."

For the next couple of weeks, Baraghani is taking a much-needed break from the limelight before ramping up again. He's back at home making the most of family time, taking advantage of the seasonal produce at farmers markets and looking to grow his extensive mortar and pestle collection at flea markets in San Francisco. "I'm gonna call out my mother in this article. I can't believe after all this time, she's only just pulled out this big, beautiful brass mortar and pestle that's over 90 years old!" Baraghani laughs. "It was my great-grandmother's when she passed away six years ago. My aunt who's here from Canada brought this from Iran for my mother to keep, and it's been hiding in the garage all this time."

Baraghani is discreet about future projects. "I'm not a horoscopes person, but I know this much about my Sagittarius sign: I don't want to be limited to one thing. I'm going back to video later down the line and I'll be working on another book eventually," he says. "It sounds like I've got all the pieces together, but the truth is that I'm still trying to figure things out. It's more about continuing, evolving, taking these different turns, seeing what happens and embracing those changes. All I can do to move through them is to try to set my doubts aside, get back to the kitchen, and cook."

> "All I can do is to try to set my doubts aside, get back to the kitchen, and cook."

FEATURES

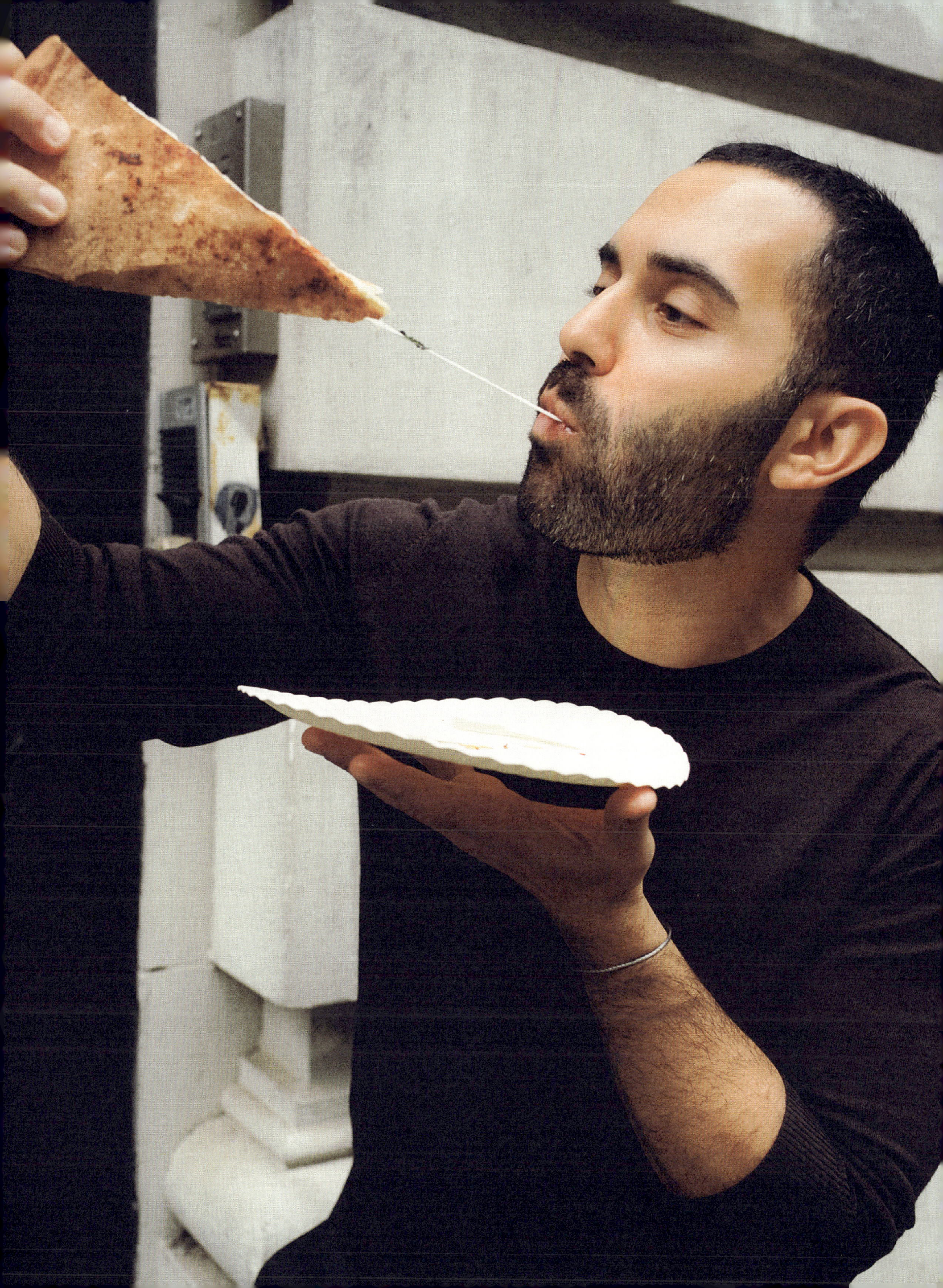

STUDIO VISIT:

A cabin in the Cascade Mountains houses a hermetic artist — and her extraordinary world of natural pigments.

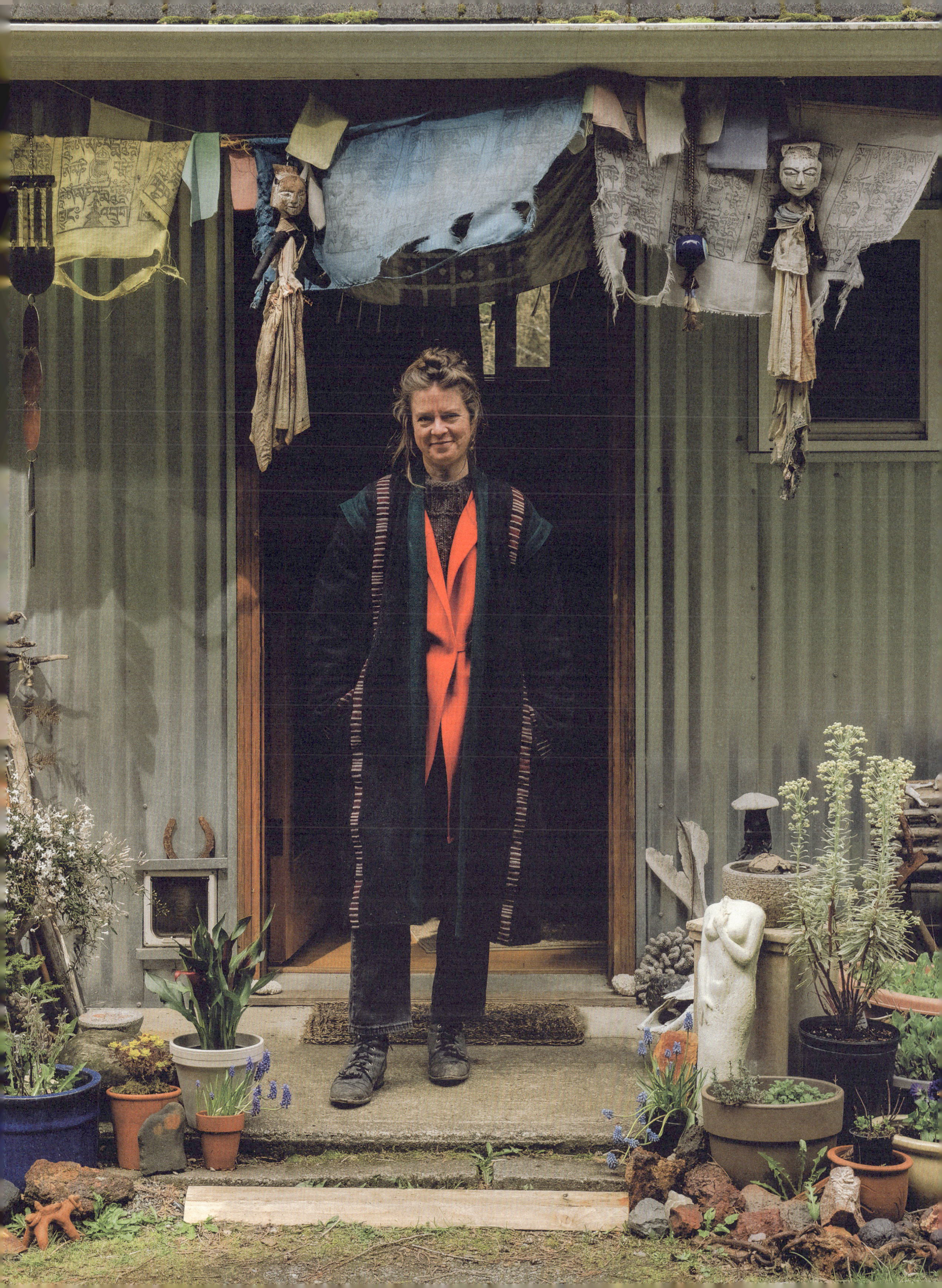

Words ALEXANDRA MARVAR
Photos ARMIN TEHRANI

About five miles from the United States–Canada border, across the vineyards and raspberry barrens and the oxbow bends of Washington state's Nooksack River, a dead-end road hangs a sharp left, sending me in the direction of artist Heidi Gustafson's cabin. A view of snow-capped Mount Baker (or, in Nooksack, *Kollia-Kulshan*—"white, shining, steep mountain") disappears behind the trees as I get deep into its foothills.

In the shade of a woodland is Gustafson's one-story, three-room home, formerly a music studio. From the outside, it looks charmingly cobbled together, dressed up with sage and dandelions and a sun-faded garland of prayer flags. One would never guess it houses the world's best known, broadest reaching and most carefully amassed collection of natural pigments—a rainbow-colored assortment of dust ground from an ancient iron-based, oxygen-rich substance called ochre.

It's April—perhaps the very first springlike weekend of the season—and when I pull into Gustafson's driveway, she is hanging her sweaters among the trees to air out. An artist trained in interdisciplinary sculpture at the Maryland Institute College of Art in Baltimore, she came back home to the West Coast a little more than a decade ago to earn her master's in philosophy, cosmology and consciousness at the California Institute of Integral Studies. As she tells it, she stumbled onto her work with pigments

(opposite) A notebook saturated with ochres in Gustafson's studio. In *Book of Earth*, Gustafson expresses her love for ochre and details how it permeates her life in unexpected ways. "I love American superstar Cardi B's way of saying 'okurrrrrr,'" she quips.

while in a different plane of consciousness, during meditation: "Ochre came in pretty loud," she tells me. She emerged from that initial encounter with one haunting question: *What the fuck is ochre?*

Gustafson has spent the decade since devoted to addressing that question and the myriad tangential lines of inquiry that have cropped up in its wake. Connecting the dots between ochre's historical, scientific, symbolic and sacred properties, she has proceeded to trace the substance's uses, from ancient Egyptian funerary texts to 100,000-year-old South African cave paintings, and from Indigenous Mexican healing traditions to the manufacturing processes of Taiwanese industrial plants.

Rocks and soil have life and depth beyond most people's wildest imaginations, Gustafson says, and she hopes her work might help people understand and regard the planet differently—more deeply—down to its pulsing iron core. This year, she released the hardcover *Book of Earth: A Guide to Ochre, Pigment, and Raw Colors*—a vivid, large-format homage to these earthy tones in all their history and complexity.

Gradually, her work and her home have become inseparable. Even Gustafson's refrigerator, just inside the front door, has become an art installation, showcasing masterworks of correspondence: a note scrawled on a Ziploc bag of quicksand; a letter from an alchemist, written on a dried kombucha mother that looks and feels like an ancient scroll; various blots of homemade ink on handcrafted paper.

"These are letters from people when they send me ochres," she says. "There are some people I've never met, and their ochres—," she gestures beyond into her expansive studio space, at her collection that fills shelves along the walls, "—are like a way of saying 'hi' through the land." Gustafson shows me around the studio, pointing out ochres from all over the world: shelf upon shelf of jars, bowls, nubs, bricks, lumps and balls of ochre that she has either foraged herself or that have been sent to her, such as a sample of kokowai red clay ochre from New Zealand. "The texture, the smell … they tell you a lot about where they're from," she says, picking up an orange and white chunk of rock sent to her by a soil scientist in São Paulo, and holding it to her nose. "It smells just like kids' tempera paint."

A small trace of every one of these ochres also makes its way onto a special set of shelves—the collection, where Gustafson showcases an earth-tones rainbow of hand-ground colored powders in tiny, meticulously labeled glass vials. The samples on these shelves number well into the hundreds.

Light is streaming in through the window and falling across Gustafson's large wooden desk and all the trays of pigment on it that she has arranged by color. There's a collection of slate-blue and gray samples, the star of which is an iridescent botryoidal hematite, with its spooky, oil-slick rainbow of thin-film interference. In a tray of white pigments are pearls, bones and sand dollars. "And coyote poop," she points out, "which has lots of calcium carbonate from bones."

In a tray of bright blues, there's an oblong, brown object that looks out of place. Introduced to her by another pigment forager, this special specimen is a fossilized spruce cone formed when a tsunami felled a swath of forest on the Oregon coast, burying it in tidal mud. "All their phosphorus, their life force, got trapped in the cones, and then, over time, they mineralized," Gustafson

WISP
CREATU

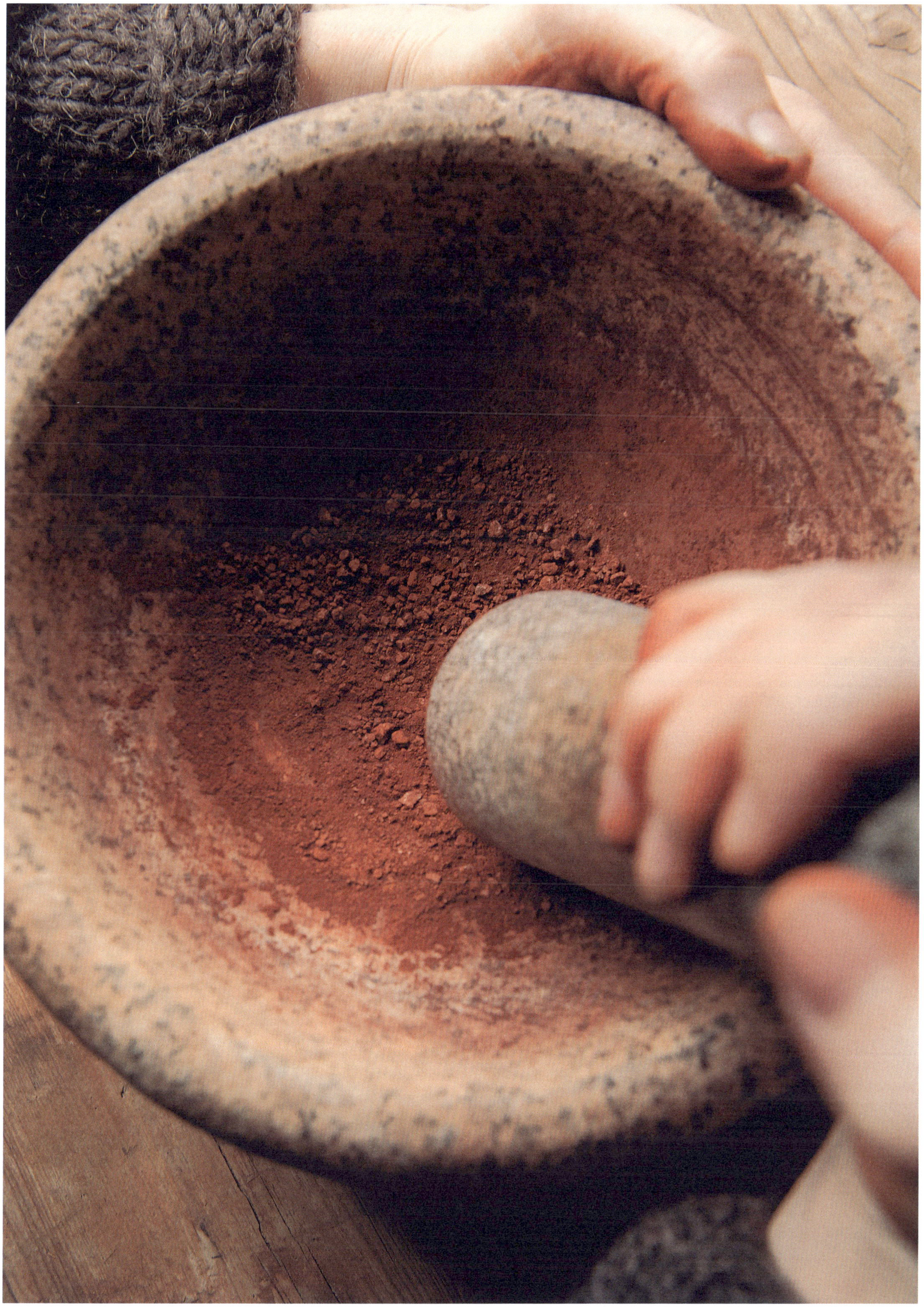

" Ochres are like a way of saying 'hi' through the land."

explains. She snaps the tiny spruce cone cleanly in half, revealing a bright cerulean iron phosphate pigment—vivianite—at its center.[1] "They just look like nothing in the mud," she says, putting one in my hand. Its existence makes the geological feat of a diamond seem almost banal. "This is tsunami power that makes that," she says.

A selection of ochres are sequestered in a special, shrine-like display, off limits for photographs. These "more potentiated" ochres are special to Gustafson, connected to places and memories or that she feels have a particular spiritual energy about them. They're surrounded by offerings: feathers, dried herbs, flickering votives.

The long game for this project goes far above and beyond the walls of Gustafson's cabin. She flips through a binder of sketches and collages—inspiration images for a brick-and-mortar ochre sanctuary with hand-formed niches, full of colors. A dynamic installation like this will one day, she hopes, house her council of ochres.

But for now, she is continuing with her "subtle activism" for a shift in awareness as to where color comes from, along with assisting any artist trying to connect with pigments from their own sacred places or ancestral lands—a foundational purpose of her work. Gustafson hopes that her work will also interest "people that are culturally not connected to ochres anymore, to help them have more awareness around the importance and significance of them." "If we don't know that," she asks, "how can we protect them? And how can we help Indigenous people protect them?"

"There's a fine line," she adds. "I don't want to tell ochre stories that aren't mine to tell. But the fact that ochre is ubiquitously used everywhere without any understanding of its connection to place: We need to talk about that."

---

(1) In *Book of Earth*, Gustafson describes vivianite, or blue ochre, as "a diva" due the rapid transformations that can occur on contact with fingers, oil, heat and light. Cerulean turns deep blue within a matter of hours, and can eventually turn dark green and matte black.

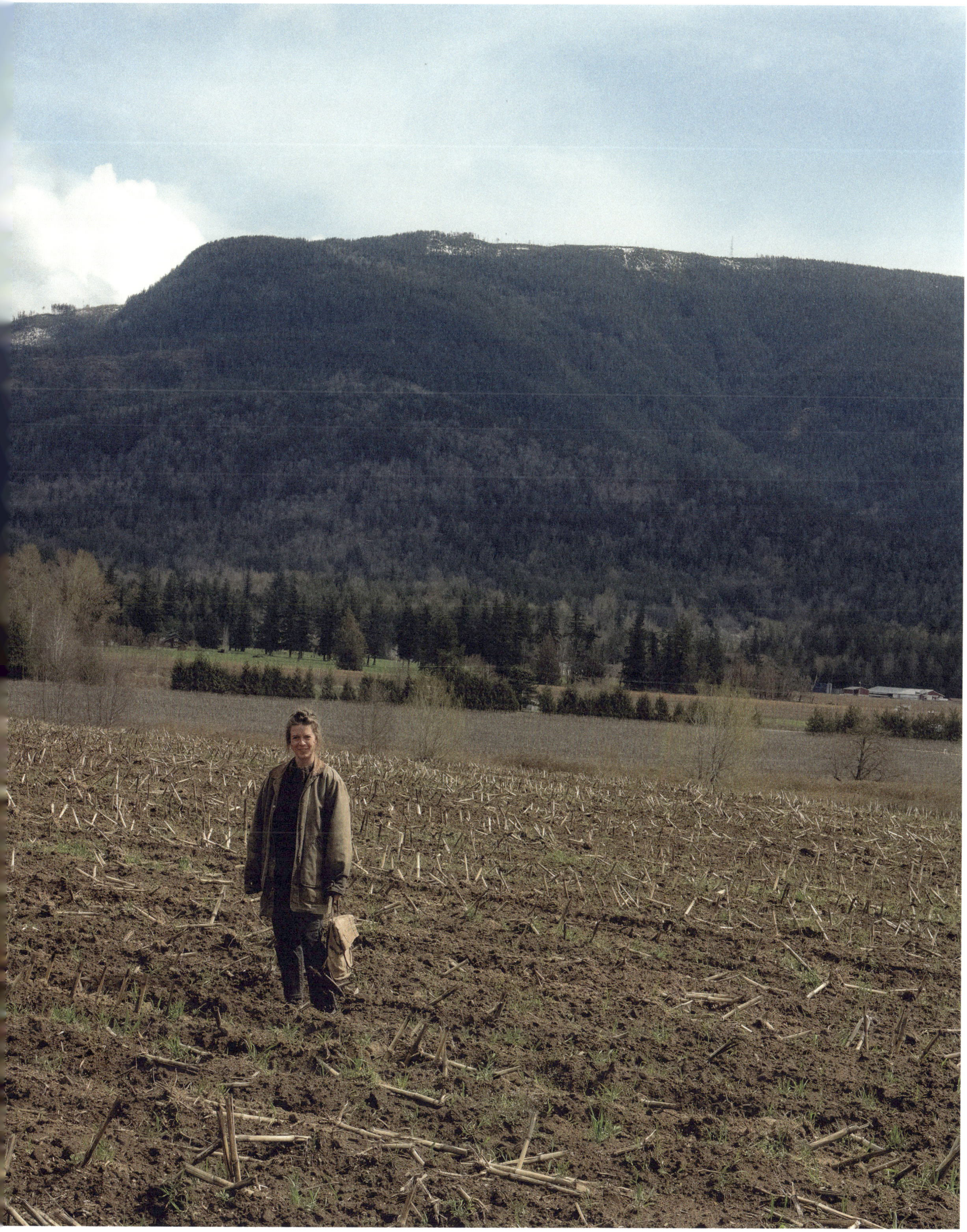

Words
ROBERT ITO

JEN NY

Photography
KOURTNEY KYUNG SMITH

ODELL

THE ACCLAIMED AUTHOR IN SEARCH OF LOST TIME.

76 FEATURES

Jenny Odell has been busy lately contemplating time, not so much about how we could use it more productively, but how time, in the hands of taskmasters throughout history, has been used against us. In her latest book, *Saving Time: Discovering a Life Beyond the Clock*, Odell discusses how time, something that most of us always figured was just sort of here, ticking away, was actually created and commodified by capitalism to, among other things, squeeze every possible bit of blood, sweat and labor out of workers.

Saving Time stands in stark contrast to most business and self-help books with similar titles, the sorts of hectoring screeds that promise to show readers how to increase their productivity by, say, "working smarter, not harder." Similarly, Odell herself is just about as far from the so-called "productivity bros" (her term) who write those sorts of books as one can imagine: She's a celebrated and gifted author, an artist and an intellectual who has written a wide-ranging book about moss and clocks, 1920s "personal efficiency" manuals and store-bought beans, that's nearly impossible to put down.

From her home in the Grand Lake neighborhood of Oakland, a "Long Lost Oakland" poster on the wall behind her,[1] Odell speaks to me about *Saving Time*, explaining how time is so different for the rich guy and his not-so-rich servant; the horrible roots behind the saying "time is money"; and why some of her best work comes when she looks like she's not working at all.

RI: How did this book come to be?

JO: There were a bunch of different strands of beginnings that came together in this book. In *How to Do Nothing*, there's an implicit argument that not all time should be money.[2] That it would be great if not all time *seemed* like money. I began to notice that a lot of reactions to that book would center on time, about not having control of one's time, and not having enough of it. Someone might be sympathetic to the arguments in the book, but timewise, didn't really know how they could make it work.

So that furthered the path that I was already on—thinking about time. And some of it just came from personal experience: I felt like *I* was always running out of time, or I was feeling a sense of dread regarding the climate, or I was worried about aging. I didn't feel good when I was thinking about time, and my recurring anxiety dreams were always about running out of it.

RI: There are many books about maximizing time, which is what people might think your book is about. Where do you see *Saving Time* in relation to those sorts of self-help manuals?

JO: When I was looking at traditional time management books, they never mentioned your employer. The books aimed at women didn't mention gender hierarchy so much. Typically, the scope of

(1) Illustrated by Liam O'Donoghue and T.L. Simons, the map features places and wildlife that no longer exist in the city, including the Berkeley kangaroo rat. Odell mentions the poster in *How to Do Nothing*.

(2) Published in 2019, *How to Do Nothing: Resisting the Attention Economy* discusses the importance of doing nothing and the value of being alone with one's thoughts in our internet-obsessed world.

KINFOLK

the problem is pretty local: You are a person in some set of circumstances, and you need to use your time more efficiently. But the question of *why* you feel like you're running out of time is left out. I was trying to zoom out from that—to look at reasons beyond the individual about why they might be having a painful relationship to time.

And I like to think of my book as being a bit more forgiving. Some of those books can feel punitive, right? Like, *you're* not doing a good enough job with your time. But depending on your circumstances, there are ways in which this is not necessarily your fault. This might not be a question of you not effectively using your time, but a question of the larger hierarchies and structures of power that you are embedded in.

RI: Not to be flip, but how did you find the time to write a book?

JO: I actually was teaching for the majority of the time that I was writing it.[3] But probably one of the most important factors was that I don't have children, and the sharing of household duties with my boyfriend is very equitable. There were points, especially at the very end—when I had cups all over my desk and everything was a mess—where he was definitely picking up the slack.

> " It was kind of mind-bending to me that time is actually not this thing that we all take for granted."

It's a little hard to measure how much time it took, because a lot of the writing for me happens in my head when I'm walking around and I'm off the clock. With this book, in particular, I really came to appreciate how much of what we would call writing actually happens for me in conversation with other people. It looks like I'm just hanging out with friends, but it makes it into the book.

RI: Tell me more about the title. The book isn't really about saving time in a sort of hyperefficient, capitalist productivity sort of way.

JO: Yeah, it's a little tongue-in-cheek, because while it does seem to invoke those types of books, it's really referring more to the idea of saving different senses of time. In the past, I've thought about saving these different notions of time the same way that seeds are saved in a seed bank. When I first started writing, I was thinking about that really punitive clock time or labor time as an invasive species of time that grew out of a particular historical context and then spread around. So when I say "saving time," I'm also referring to this idea of rescuing notions of time that are endangered or drowned out by this one specific way of thinking about time.

(3) Odell was an adjunct lecturer in Art Practice at Stanford University from 2013 to 2021. Her teaching and work as an artist reflects her interest in the ecology of images created by networks and phones, with projects often using secondhand imagery from Google Maps, YouTube and Craigslist.

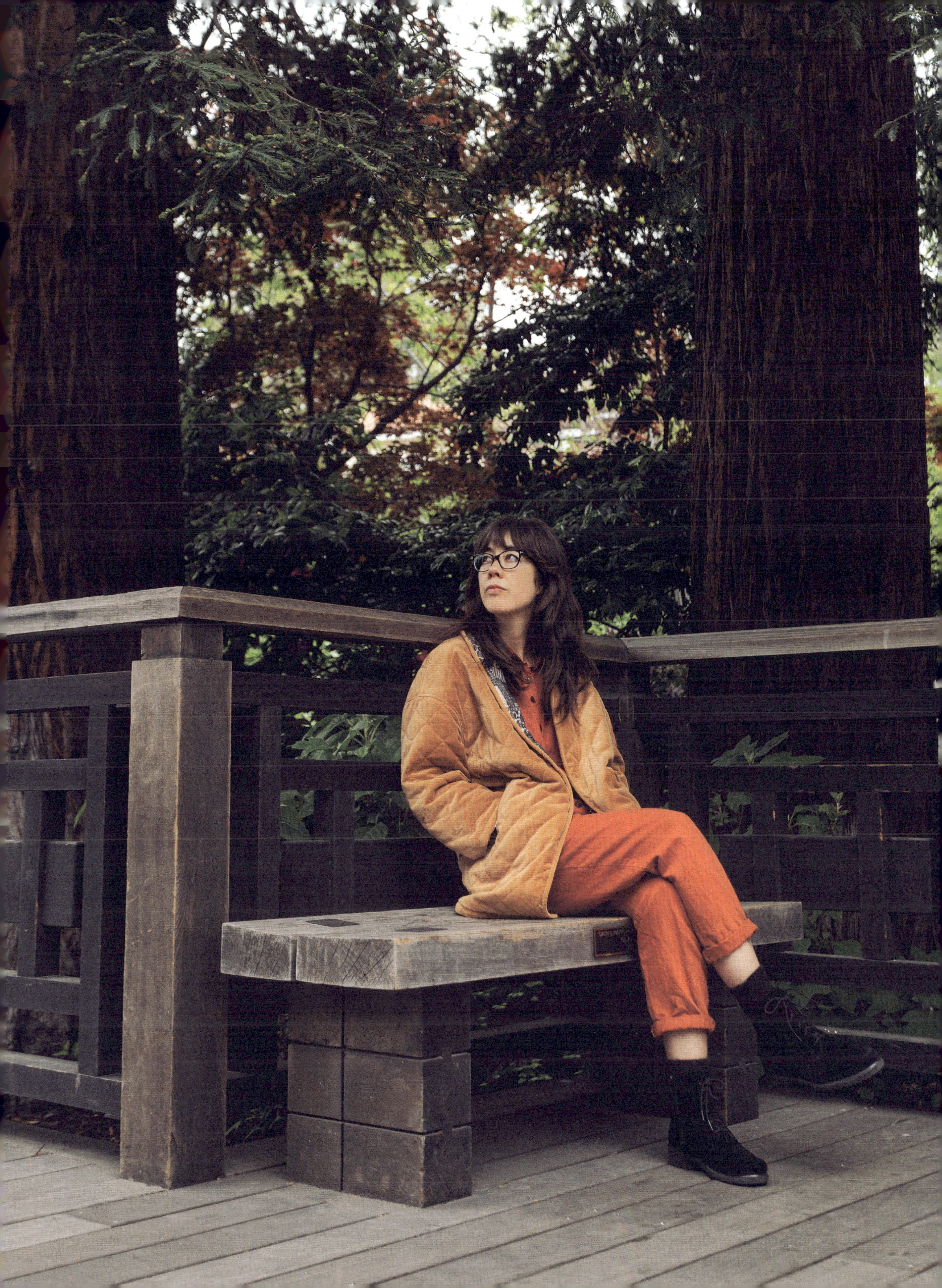

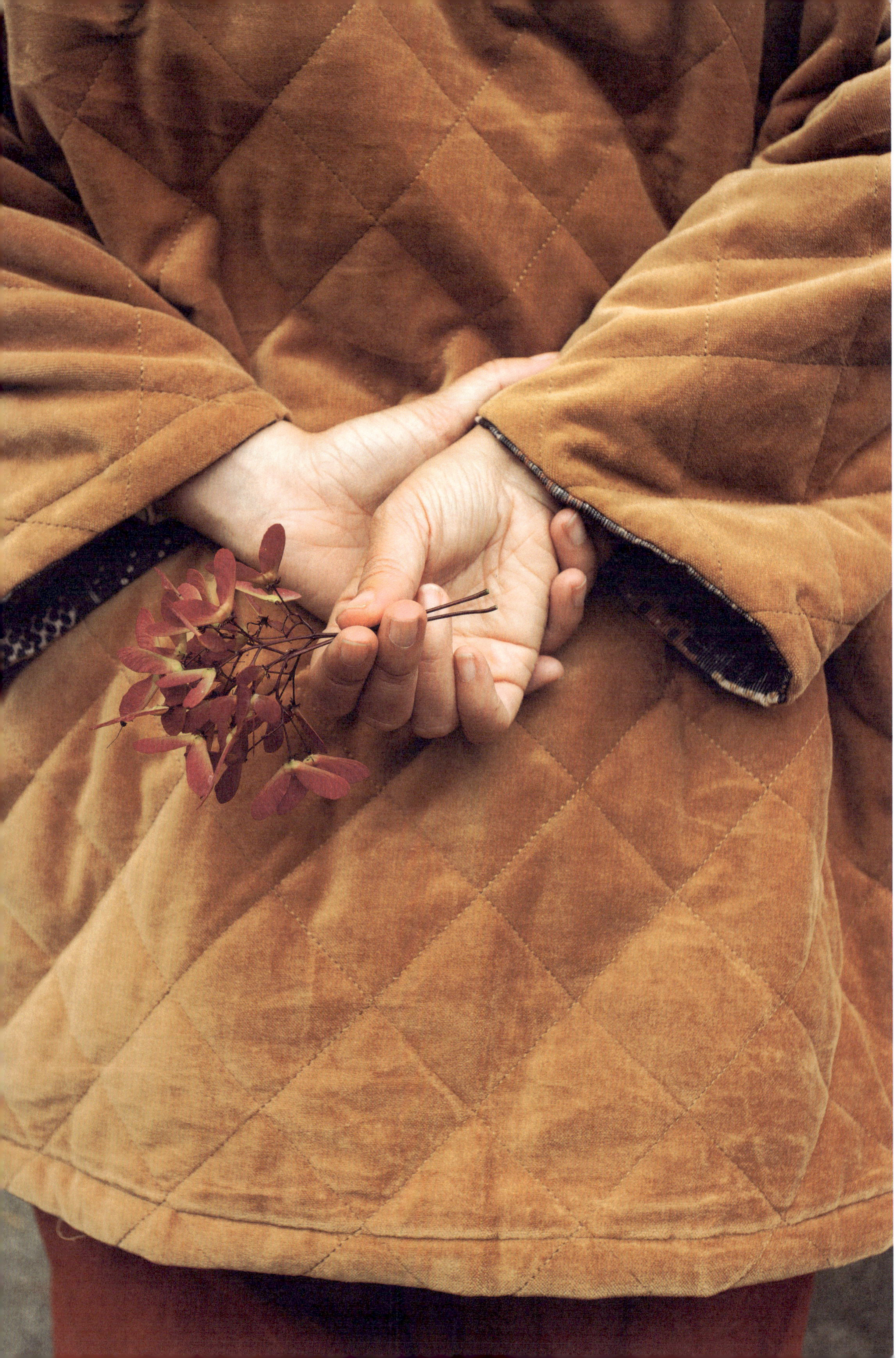

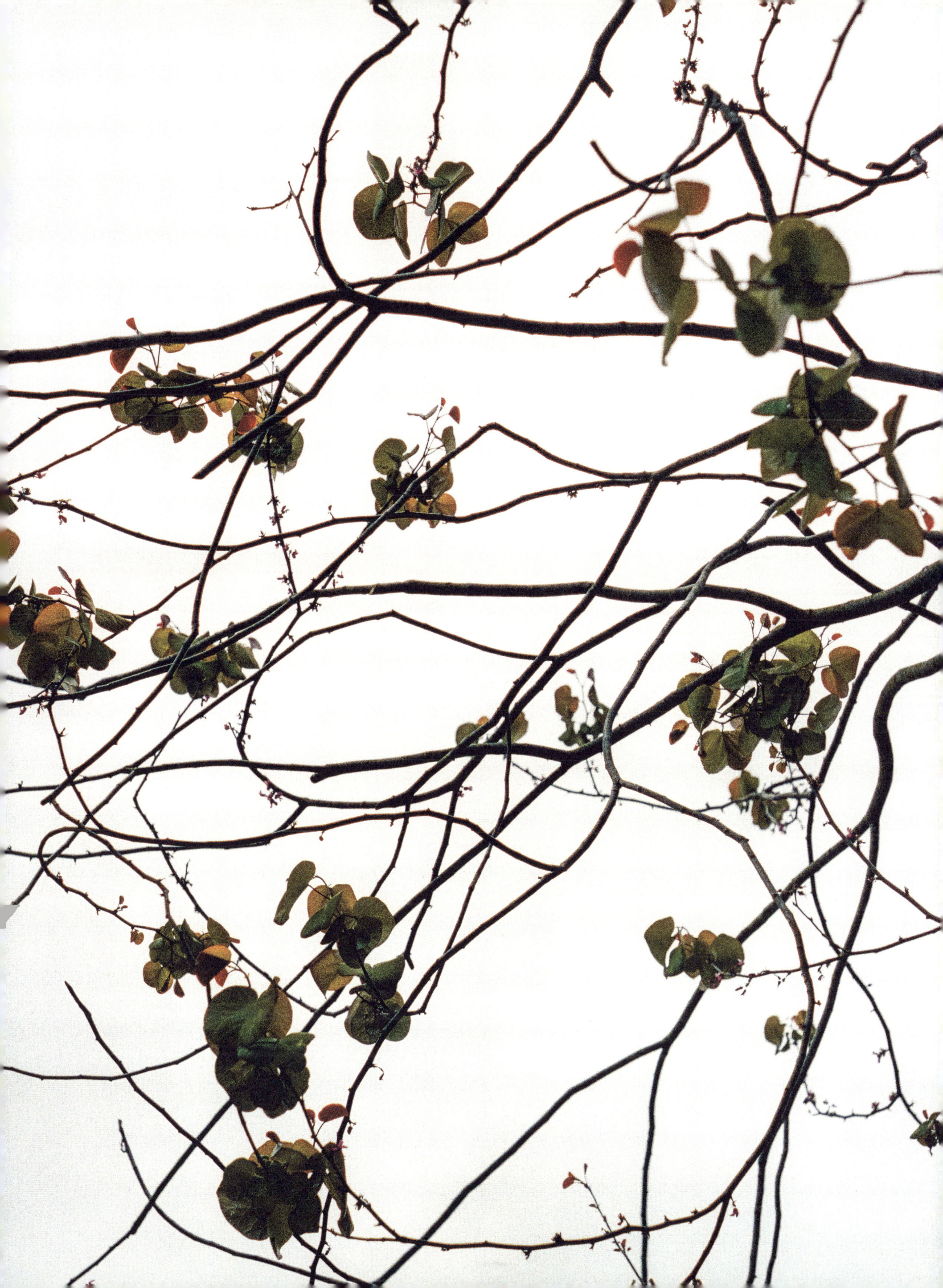

RI: You write about how time has become commodified to service this push to make people work faster and harder. But has the slow movement become commodified too?

JO: I think slowness is best understood in a wider framework that is at odds with the common notion that everything is getting faster. That's something that you hear a lot: that everything's getting faster for everyone, uniformly. But as [author and academic] Sarah Sharma[4] wondered, what about the cab driver who's waiting for the jet-setting guy? A person who's acting at the behest of someone else sometimes has to speed up, other times they have to slow down, and whether or not you have power in any situation will affect whether you have the power to make your time feel fast or slow. In that framework, it's easy to understand how something like slowness could become a luxury. Someone with money, for example, can pay for the early boarding on a plane. They can also pay to go to a spa. Or they can pay to go to an organic farm where things are made very slowly. Basically, they can have it be any way that they want. For me, that helps explain what otherwise seems like a paradox: that slowness would become something that's actually just part of the same buying and selling of experiences.

RI: Why do you think people would try to sell the notion of slowness or the product of slowness? Or is it just the nature of capitalism that you're going to try to sell anything if you can?

JO: You know, I'm not actually sure. But I think there are a lot of people who would like to slow down. It feels more humane. That impulse is something that is very real. And capitalism is so good at identifying all kinds of desire, even if they're just starting to emerge, and sort of pouncing on them. And I think that's probably what happened with slowness.

(4) Sharma is a professor of media theory at the University of Toronto and author of the book *In the Meantime: Temporality and Cultural Politics.*
(5) The index of *Saving Time* runs 16 pages, with citations ranging from "Accounting for Slavery (Rosenthal)" to "Zuckerberg, Mark."

RI: You clearly did a lot of research for the book.[5] What were some of the more surprising things you learned?

JO: It was a horrible surprise, but I learned that the earliest documents that we would call spreadsheets were used on plantations. And I was surprised by some of the anecdotes about clashes between colonists and colonized people, and how contested time was then. There were these moments where the 24-hour day and the seven-day week with the Sabbath were not givens. It was kind of mind-bending to me that time is actually not this thing that we all take for granted. Some of the things that I learned about geology were also very surprising to me—that that is time too, one that the clock on my wall has no authority over.

I was really taken with some of the examples of other kinds of timing. Vine Deloria Jr.[6] has an example of tribes along the Missouri River who would plant corn and then retreat to the mountains for the summer. They "abandoned" the corn, but once the seed pods of a certain type of plant on the mountain reached a certain size, that was their cue to go down and get the corn. That's an extremely minute, detailed way of timing something, but it's so different from the clock-based notion that all time is the same.

> "There are a lot of people who would like to slow down. It feels more humane."

RI: So how do we get out from under this oppressive clock?

JO: There are different answers based on the position that you occupy. For someone who could potentially have control over their time, but maybe feels like they don't because they're overextended, I feel like, and I say this in the book, they should experiment with what feels like mediocrity.

But for the folks who don't have as much control over their time, I think we've had the answer to that for a long time: workplace organizing, and policies that would open up time for people, like paid leave. Universal Basic Income is an interesting example, and very tied to the idea of time as money.

In Matthew Desmond's new book, *Poverty, by America*, he interviews someone who's working two jobs and barely has enough time to sleep, and no time to spend with his family or his friends. He joins the Fight for $15 campaign for minimum wage, and because of their successes, he gets more time. But the only way for him to do that was to address the fact that all of his time was being controlled by his situation.

(6) The Sioux lawyer was an activist for Native American rights and author of the 1969 book *Custer Died for Your Sins*, which helped attract national attention to Native American issues.

(7) Launched in 2012, the US-based movement pushed for a federal minimum wage of $15 an hour.

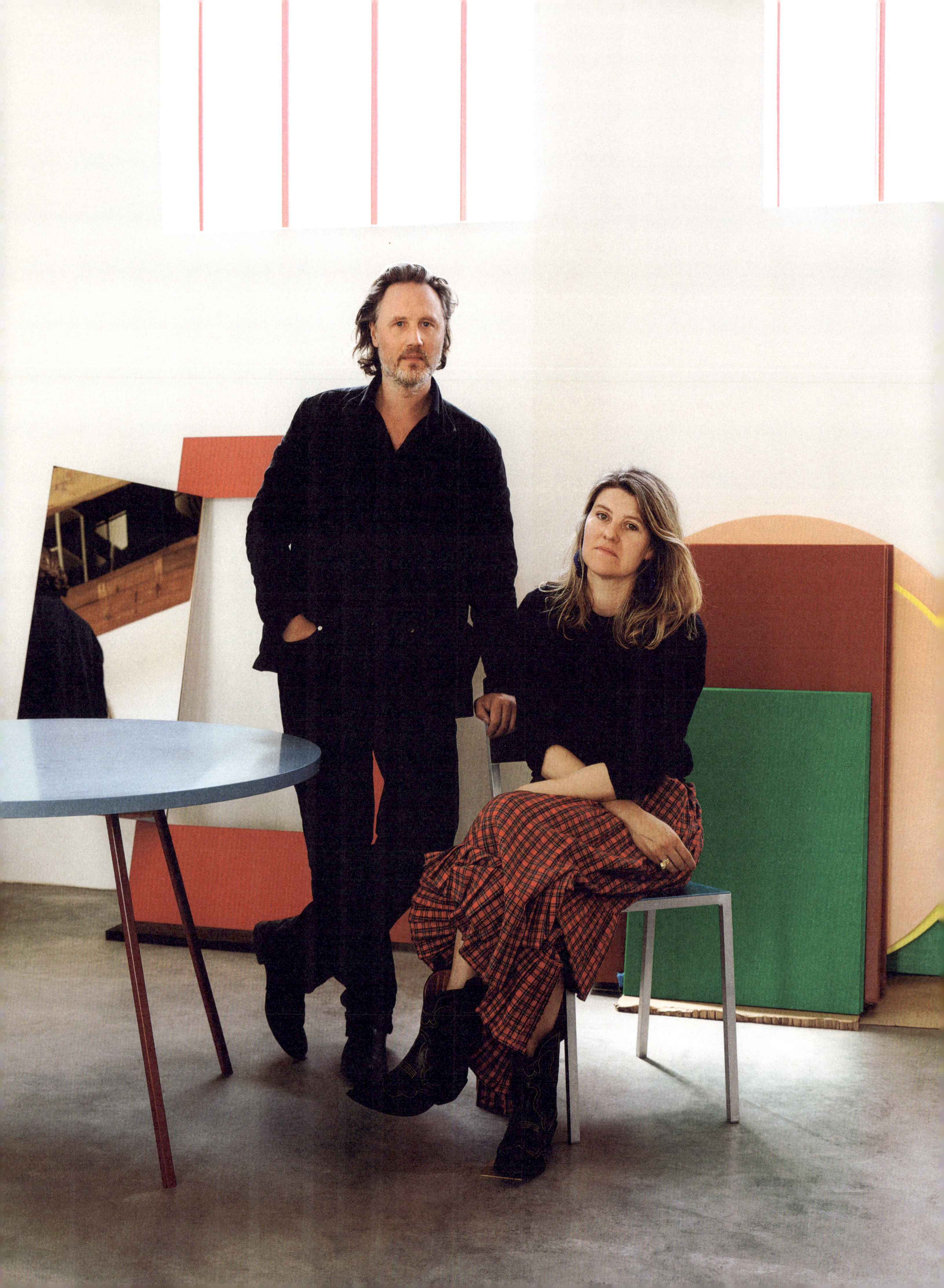

Words BENJAMIN DANE

At Work *With* MULLER VAN SEVEREN

How a home renovation birthed one of Europe's most distinguished design duos.

Photos CECILIE JEGSEN

Muller Van Severen has mushroomed from a make-do moment at home into a commercially successful design studio. *Benjamin Dane* meets the founders where it all began—at the bottom of their garden.

There are only a few dozen steps between the blue front door of Fien Muller and Hannes Van Severen's home and the entrance of their acclaimed studio, Muller Van Severen. Across a courtyard, overlooking the garden, an old orangery has been transformed into a two-story office and atelier for the designers and their two assistants.

It was architect Élise Van Thuyne who helped the couple renovate the studio, which is located just outside of Ghent, Belgium, when they moved into the house back in 2008, adding bright, red-framed floor-to-ceiling windows to let in more light. The interior was split into two—one half for desk work and the other for the production of the colorful line of furniture and objects that Muller Van Severen has been creating since 2011.

"From nine to five—once we've dropped off our two daughters at school—we're in the studio," says Van Severen, hinting at some kind of work-life balance. A few moments later, back inside the house, his wife gives them away: "Sometimes we do our drawings in here as well," says Muller.

"We both get a lot of our best ideas outside regular work hours, and we're constantly having discussions about our exhibitions."

The choice of words reveals a lot about how Muller and Van Severen see themselves: as artists first, designers second. Muller was a photographer, and Van Severen a sculptor before they both pivoted into furniture and object design. They still see themselves as creating exhibitions, not collections, and although they work with big brands such as Danish houses HAY and Kvadrat and the Tuscan ceramic manufacturer Bitossi, all of their pieces are handmade right here in the studio at the bottom of their garden, with help from local fabricators and artisans. Indeed, their work has been exhibited in museums such as the Vitra Design Museum in Germany, and both the Pompidou Center and the Musée des Arts Décoratifs in Paris. Whether it's a chair, a lamp, a shelving system or something else entirely, a Muller Van Severen design mixes minimalist, straight lines with playful colors and natural materials like aluminum, brass and marble. "Sometimes people complain about small scratches and marks," Van Severen says, "but then we try to explain that this is intentional. We feel no need to polish our products."

At Muller Van Severen, most ideas for a new design begin with the materials. They serve as a starting point from which a whole family of objects emerges. "We can become almost obsessed with a material and its possibilities," Muller says. "It often begins with a small detail or a certain profile or silhouette, and then we zoom out from there and keep on going, making as many objects as we can until we feel we can't push the idea any further."

Muller and Van Severen met in a sculpting class while studying at Sint-Lucas art school in Ghent. After graduation, they both pursued their own individual careers and mediums as artists, and while they'd often discussed working together, the right occasion hadn't presented itself. This changed, however, when they moved into their current home. At the time, they'd been together as a couple for seven years. While renovating, they found themselves in need of a lamp over their new kitchen table—and

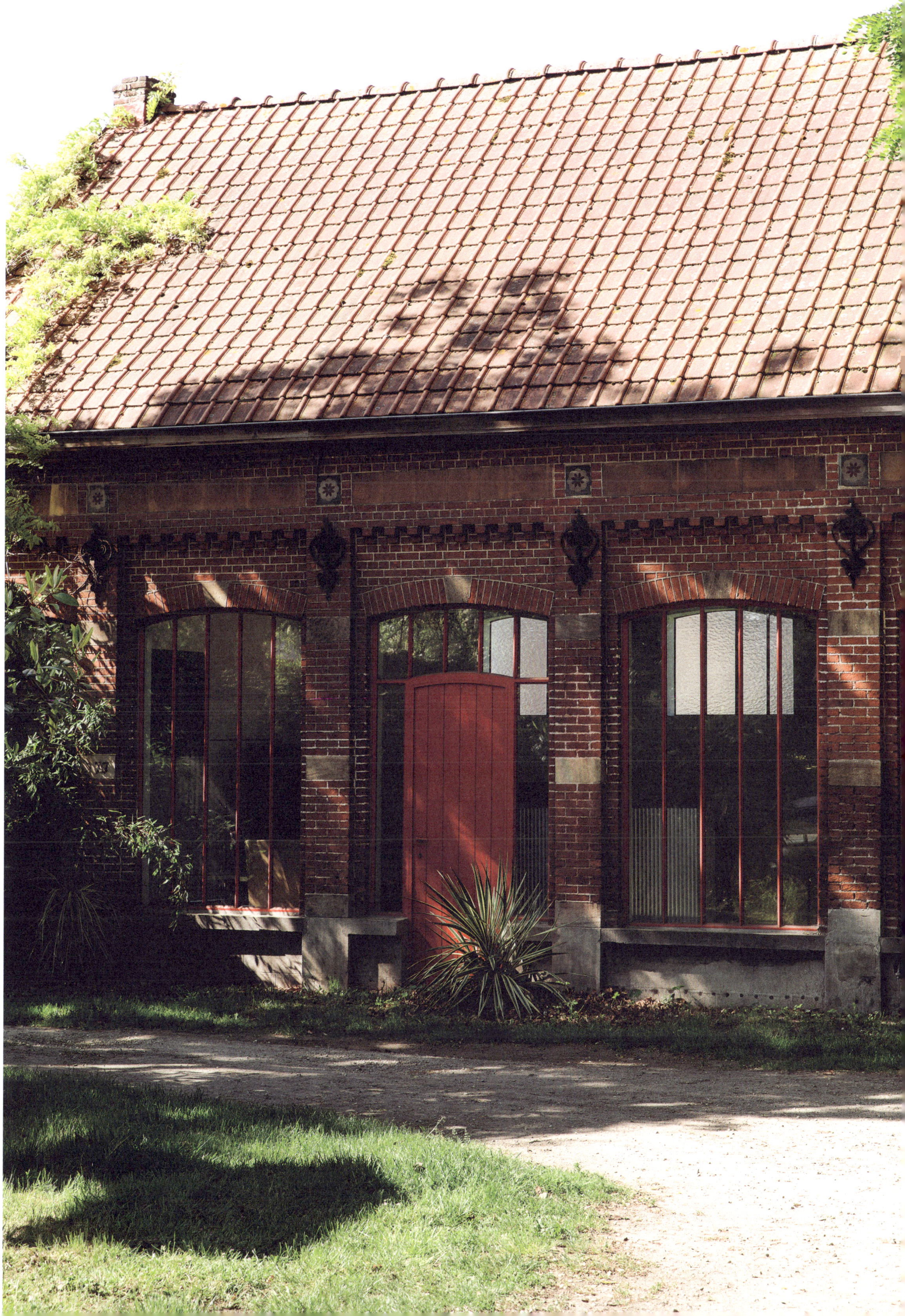

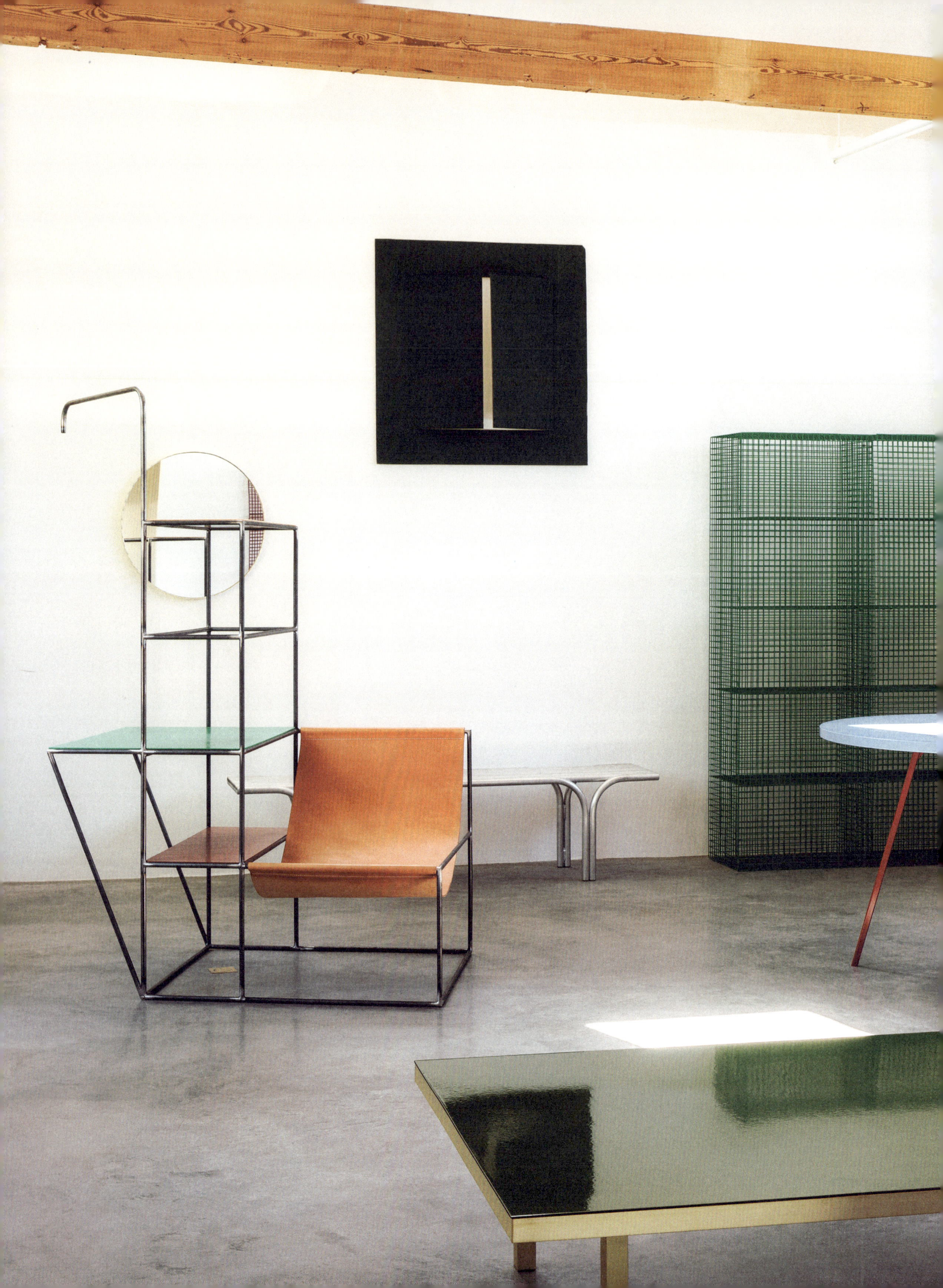

(opposite)   Installation S—a combined seat, rack, table and lamp—is part of the series that Muller Van Severen first presented in 2012 at the Biennale Interieur in Kortrijk, Belgium.

also discovered that there was no electrical wiring in the ceiling. "We decided to solve the problem by making a cantilever lamp together," says Muller.

It was an idea that developed into Muller Van Severen's first real product design, a polyethylene table with a metal tube stuck into one of the legs that extends over the table and curves into a lamp; Muller calls it "a romantic touch on an otherwise very strict object." They named it "table + lamp," and the piece became part of their first exhibition at the Antwerp gallery Valerie Traan in 2011. "Designing furniture and objects felt liberating for both of us," Van Severen says. "Where others might have felt confined by the boundaries of a design brief, we thrived in creating objects that had to have an actual function."

There was never a Muller Van Severen business plan or any overarching goals, but continuing to work together just felt natural—almost symbiotic. "In the beginning, it was more of a side project next to our respective careers, but it quickly became our main thing when our designs began to resonate with people," Muller explains. Their breakthrough came only a year later, in 2012, when curator and designer Lowie Vermeersch snuck the duo into the Biennale Interieur in Kortrijk—Belgium's leading interior design event—alongside internationally renowned names. They showed a series of works that—like "table + lamp"—combined two or more functions into one design object, including a bookcase with attached seating in the bright colors that have since come to define Muller Van Severen's work.

"We consider color almost as a material in its own right," Van Severen says. "It's always a key element when we start working on a design, and never something that we just decide afterward." "I also think that we always strive to find a balance between the masculine and feminine," Muller adds. "We like to describe our work as cool and technical and warm and romantic at the same time, and that can be achieved, for instance, by combining bright colors with something like raw steel."

Both Muller and Van Severen come from creative families and have always been surrounded by art and design. Muller was born into a family of artists and art collectors, and Van Severen is the son of well-known Belgian furniture designer and interior architect Maarten Van Severen, who worked for Vitra, among others.[1] "For me, studying arts just seemed the most normal thing I could possibly do," says Van Severen. "As I get older, I feel that I resemble my parents more and more," Muller adds. "The way I work with color and shapes today was cultivated in my childhood where I grew up in a very baroque, colorful and eclectic home, while Hannes grew up with straight lines and not a lot of color," she adds. "It's not like we've been thinking, let's make objects where our two backgrounds come together, but I think it's just naturally evident in our work."

The couple rarely has creative disagreements about proportions, color or other aesthetic choices, but can sometimes clash on logistics or strategy. Often people ask them: "What's Hannes' role and what's Fien's?" but that's not how it works for them. Usually, one starts on a drawing, and the other expands on it, back and forth like a parlor game until a design slowly comes together.

"Of course, we do have doubts sometimes," Van Severen says, "but then it's a strength that we both have immediate access to the feedback of the other. We're both very honest, and I think it's one of the strengths of working as a couple that you can say things to each other directly." "Without having to be polite," adds Muller. They both let out a little laugh before Van Severen continues: "We trust each other blindly, and I think that's why we work together so well."

> "We feel no need to polish our products."

(1) Maarten Van Severen was a friend and collaborator with globally renowned architect Rem Koolhaas. The pair worked together on seminal projects including Maison à Bordeaux and Villa dall'Ava in France. Koolhaas has said that working with Van Severen marked "a sort of important moment in my own professional life."

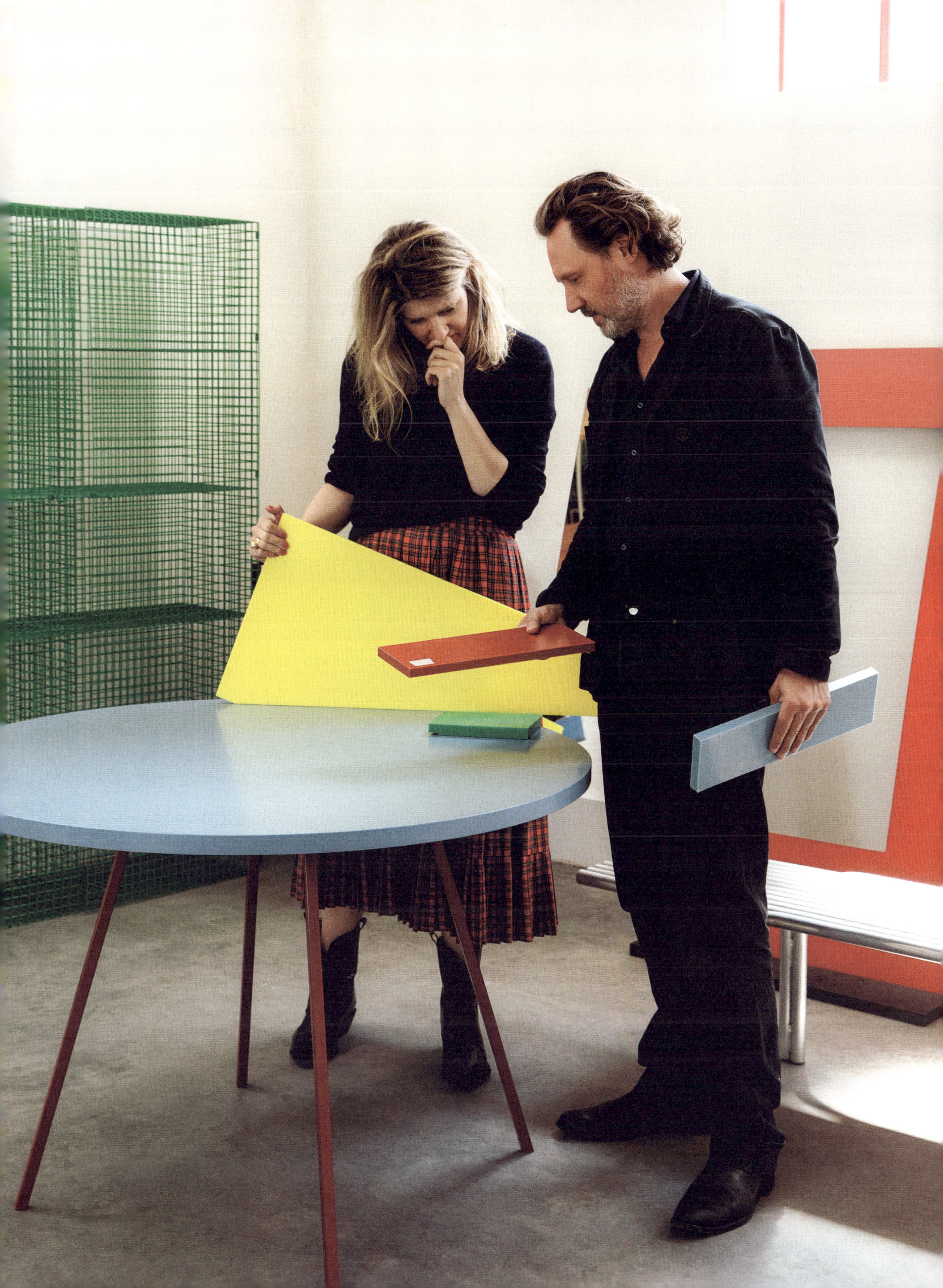

What happened to
mainstream culture?

ESSAY:
MASS DESTRUCTION

Words
ANNABEL BAI JACKSON

During the pandemic, a gentle instrumental song became ubiquitous across TikTok—used and reused to soundtrack videos of morning routines and day-in-the-life edits. With its balmy chord progression and feel-good hum, the track signaled the cultivation of an enviably tranquil mode of living, one that in itself was an aesthetic that came to dominate large swaths of the app. But despite the pervasiveness of this tune—it now accompanies over 12 million TikToks and counting—its provenance is probably obscure to the vast majority of users, including those who are familiar with its beats. It's called "Aesthetic," and it's by the musician Tollan Kim. The name probably won't ring any bells, and yet Kim's work is part of a ballooning TikTok mainstream, made up of snippets you can effortlessly—or perhaps, more accurately, mindlessly—recognize.

"polycultures"—a mainstream split into creeks.

While critics might lament the wane in watercooler TV and must-have albums, this shift has a more complicated impact on artists. Success in the mainstream is inevitably tied to TV commissioners, A&R scouts and marketing executives. But up-and-comers wanting to get spotted no longer have to fight through these traditional, often exclusionary corridors of power: Digital pathways offer a bypass. One genre that has massively benefited from this is lo-fi, defined by Jack Brophy—the founder of lo-fi music label the Jazz Hop Café—as a minimalist sound featuring synthetic beats and sampled melodies, made by so-called "bedroom producers." Mostly created independently without the backing of studio execs, lo-fi tracks have exploded across the internet, with the Jazz Hop Café's YouTube channel amassing 109 million

" Artists have millions of monthly streams, yet only a couple of thousand followers on social media."

The contradiction at the heart of Tollan Kim's success—millions of people know his song, but he couldn't be further from a household name—represents a flux in the thorny, ill-defined category of "the mainstream." For years, journalists have been anxiously diagnosing its terminal decline, identifying the internet as the guilty party.[1] Algorithmic platforms including Spotify, TikTok and YouTube at once niche-ify our listening interests, pushing us into ever-shrinking, personalized echo chambers, and disperse them over a broader range of options—making musicians like Kim achieve incredible numeric success, without the qualitative cultural capital to go along with it. Meanwhile, streaming services like Netflix and Prime pump out more content than we could possibly consume, dramatically lessening the chances that a single show becomes a unanimous cultural touchstone. We see a "monoculture" fragment into

views since it launched in 2015. But circumventing one path to success means wrestling with another.[2] For Brophy, musicians have now become "a slave to algorithms." "Artists are often left baffled by the fact that they have millions of monthly streams, yet only a couple of thousand followers on social media," he says. "And they're not likely to be selling out a tour anytime soon, either."

(1) In a 2019 article, *The Guardian* journalist Simon Reynolds wrote that streaming has killed the mainstream. "While the clock and the calendar continue to plod forward in their steadfast and remorseless way, what you could call 'culture-time' feels like it's become unmoored and meandering," he wrote.

(2) Conversely, many famous musicians are requested by their labels to make lo-fi TikToks: Over just a few weeks in early 2022, FKA twigs, Halsey, Charli XCX and Florence Welch protested at their respective labels' insistence that they should fabricate a viral moment, incidentally going viral in the process.

Lo-fi, and other artistic products of the internet generation force us to reconsider how we can quantify mainstream triumph. We have statistically successful artists who are culturally obscure, with mass listenership but no real fans: If the forms of cultural and economic capital that make something mainstream have gone awry, perhaps "the mainstream" itself needs rethinking.

"The mainstream has three different meanings," according to Erik Hannerz, a sociologist at Lund University and author of *Performing Punk*. "We can talk about it as a layman's concept, describing the popular, the bland, the conventional," but within academic circles, definitions are harder to pin down. "Most, if not all contemporary research would argue that the mainstream has little, if any intrinsic meaning," given how flawed any attempt at empirical measurement would be, says Hannerz. His final definition comes from the perspective of subcultures, for whom "the mainstream only exists as a relational concept," an abstraction you define yourself against. "It has value because it's the straw man that you construct, that you distance yourself from. The distance is meaningful in itself," he says, "not the mainstream."

" The mainstream has value because it's the straw man that you construct, that you distance yourself from."

Hannerz's research sheds a different light on the journalistic elegies for the monoculture. Because it's not just punks, metalheads or cosplayers who treat the mainstream as somehow "other": Merely invoking the term in casual conversation positions you as external to it, invokes a deliberate margin of difference. If the mainstream is a concept that people almost always identify *against*, not *with*, it may be the case that it's very much alive and well—but if you're part of it, you're simply not using the language. Subcultures, Hannerz says, rely on "these maps of meanings, these rules and rituals, these representations, that tell us who we are," turning a mere viewer or listener into an insider, someone who can follow the group's "mythology." The mainstream lacks this coherent aesthetic identity, this voice from within. In some ways, this makes it an almost impossible phenomenon to talk about in a meaningful way: As soon as you've uttered it, you're outside of it.

But if the mainstream does have a solid basis, outside of being a cultural straw man, it resides in its relationship to time and space. The mainstream was once grounded in routine moments—the household TV at 9:00 p.m. on a Sunday, the watercooler in the office first thing on a Monday. There's still a huge appetite for this type of collective experience: When the British Film Institute in London hosted a midnight screening for the finale of HBO's *Succession*, tickets were snapped up pretty much instantly.[3] But by and large, with the flexibility of streaming, that shared hearth for audiences to gather around has dissipated. Even within the digital world itself, a dislocation has taken place between different platforms: Tollan Kim might have 12 million TikToks using his sound, but he only has 92,000 monthly listeners on Spotify. "Unlike the impact of punk or hip-hop culture that brought with it fashion, personality and art ... any culture with lo-fi exists entirely on the internet," Brophy says. For him, this is one of the reasons the genre "won't go down in history."

If the mainstream is indeed sputtering to a sense of an ending, this absence of carved-out moments for culture to be collectively enjoyed is certainly its biggest loss. But it might be more accurate to think about the mainstream in a slightly different way—not as a genre, or as having a discernible rise and fall, but as an event. The South Korean TV juggernaut *Squid Game*, which premiered on Netflix in 2021, was probably the last time a show ticked all the mainstream boxes on such a mass scale. It raked in the numbers, became Netflix's most-watched show ever with 1.6 billion hours of it being streamed, and bagged the cultural cachet, with publications from *The New Yorker* to *The Pittsburgh Post-Gazette* reporting on its sky-rocketing popularity. *Squid Game* also, crucially, escaped the internet that gave it its success, becoming part of the cultural conversation offline—meaning that your dad has probably heard of it.[4] If this kind of global success now only comes around every few years, the mainstream can be read as a kind of happening—a moment of cultural clarity, and a lucky glimpse at collectivity.

(3) *Succession* is not quite a watercooler show, however. Despite rave reviews for five solid years, only 2.9 million viewers tuned into the finale. It was the show's largest audience ever.

(4) In *Squid Game*, potential players are ordered to use a specific phone number to confirm their participation in the life-or-death competition. Unbeknownst to writers and producers, they used a real phone number; the owner received up to 4,000 calls and text messages in one day.

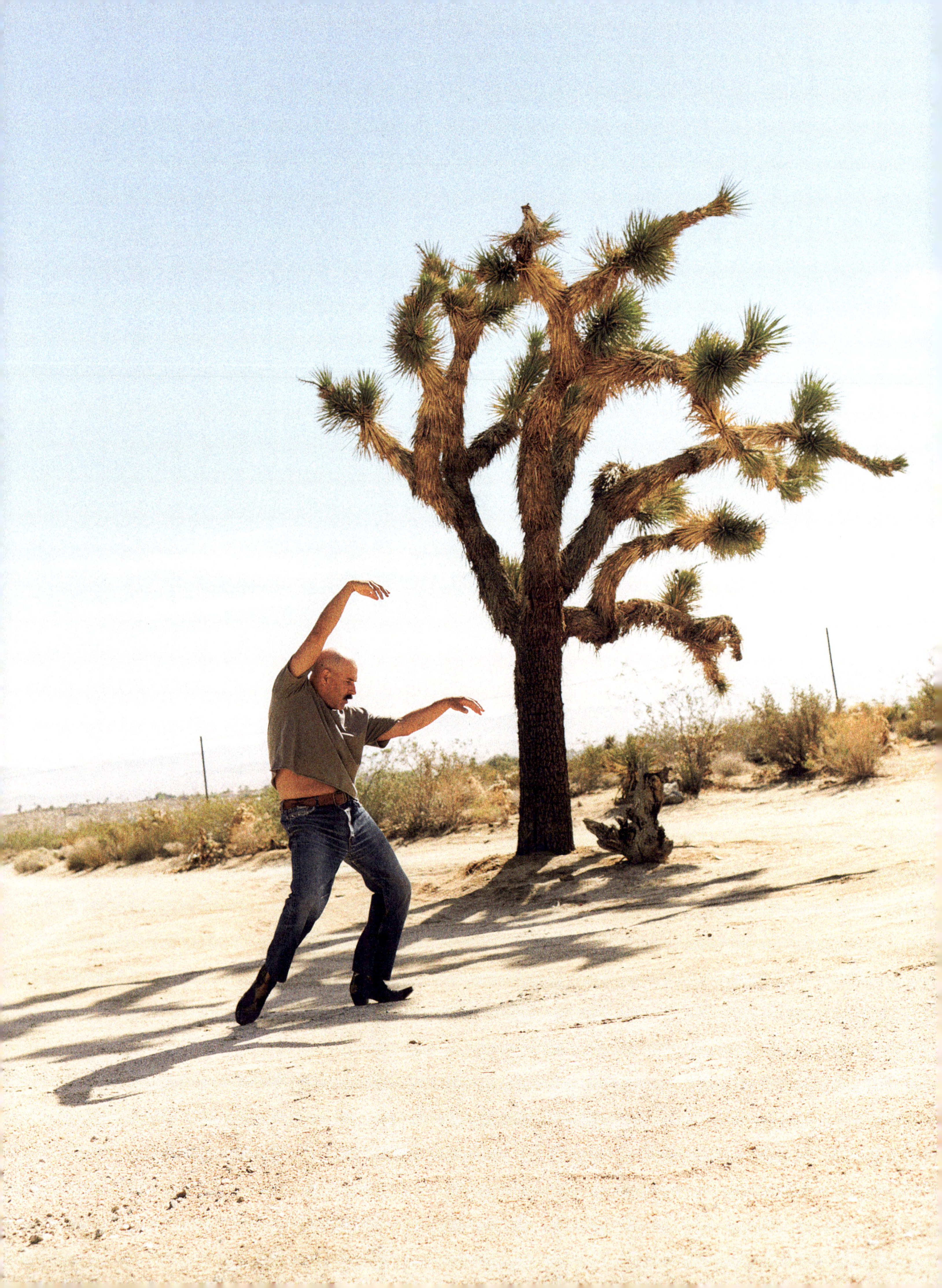

Dancing *with* RYAN HEFFINGTON

Meet the man bringing choreography, community and queer joy to the desert.

Words EMILY MAY

Photos ARIANNA LAGO

In the desert town of Twentynine Palms, choreographer RYAN HEFFINGTON is living his best life. His weird and easy dance moves might get you closer to yours too.

98　　　　　　　　　　　　　　　　　　　　　　　　FEATURES

Now renowned for high-profile projects including the music videos for Sia's 2014 hit "Chandelier" and Christine and the Queens' "La Vita Nuova," as well as feature films such as *Baby Driver* and Lin Manuel Miranda's *Tick, tick... Boom!*, choreographer Ryan Heffington first experienced dance in tap classes at a studio in his conservative Northern California hometown. "I'd ride my bike through orchards to get there, and the parking lot was next to a donkey pasture," he recalls. It was in this rural environment, where he felt like he was the only openly gay person, that the dance studio became his temple for expression. "I'm surprised how free I felt to be myself. I ruffled a few feathers, as I was pretty effeminate"—Heffington danced in every local pageant and once dressed up as Pat Benatar in "Love is a Battlefield" for Halloween—"but I don't think people understood what power I was holding through dance. I was confident, regardless of how my environment was responding to me."

Heffington's confidence to follow his own path has defined his career. Lacking a set trajectory into the performance industry, he moved to Los Angeles at 18 to experiment with movement, drugs and club culture. "I dove in hard so that I could understand who I was as an artist," he says. With no formal training, Heffington blazed his own trail, teaming up with his friend, choreographer Bubba Carr, to create cabaret shows in clubs around the city. "We made art with no money," he reminisces. "We'd duct-tape girls into material because we didn't know how to sew and we'd make wigs out of brooms and mops."

Inspired by the farcical nature of raucous talk shows like *The Jerry Springer Show* and the watermelon-smashing comedian Gallagher, Heffington and Carr's shows were "super sexual and punk," marrying absurdity with good dance technique. "We'd give each other abortions on stage and then do a tap dance number. We used all of our skills and traumas," he says, noting that both he and Carr were survivors of sexual assault. "It was cathartic and beautiful, and pushed us as artists."

As Heffington's star has ascended, a sense of absurdity has remained a key element of his choreographic commissions. His 2016 advertisement for Kenzo World, which features the actress Margaret Qualley walking out of an awards ceremony to manically frolic around the Los Angeles Music Center is a prime example. Making crazed faces in mirrors and licking the faces of stone busts, she wildly kicks, stamps and vibrates her body as if shaking off the pressure of her formal environment.

Perhaps paradoxically, Heffington draws on mundane, everyday human gestures to create his bizarre signature aesthetic. In his 2022 TED Talk, he demonstrates how for "Chandelier," he exaggerated and transformed actions such as eating with a fork, cleaning his mustache and even mimicking cockroaches crawling up walls into choreography. "It's beautiful to walk through life in the valley between reality and surrealism," he says, describing how he poses himself physical what-ifs on a daily basis. "When I'm driving, I envision getting in car wrecks. I'm intrigued by the ballet of how my body would fly through a window: Could I hold myself pushing against the wheel? Would that keep me from breaking into a million pieces? It's so exciting."

> " I ask people to bend over like they are an 80-year-old woman tying a shoelace."

Using relatable references means that Heffington's work appeals to a wide demographic, setting it apart in an art form that is often viewed as inaccessible. "Many choreographers look inward to understand their vision. I do that too, but 50% of me is always considering the audience," he says, attributing the compulsion to his background performing in clubs a mere two feet away from spectators. "I sometimes claim myself as an entertainer rather than a choreographer. That's my goal: to evoke emotion and entertain."

But Heffington doesn't just want to entertain audiences, he wants them to experience dance's cathartic and therapeutic properties for themselves. This has been the driving force behind the community-focused projects he's developed alongside his professional commissions, such as the Sweat Spot—a dance studio he ran for 10 years in LA's Silver Lake neighborhood. Inspired by several nondancers who had asked him where they could take fun classes, Heffington decided to transform a 2,200-square-foot

(left)   Heffington at his home in Twentynine Palms, California. In 2022, Heffington won an Emmy for his work choreographing three routines for the HBO series *Euphoria*; a year prior, he made his acting debut in Paul Thomas Anderson's movie *Licorice Pizza*, starring Sean Penn, Bradley Cooper and Tom Waits.

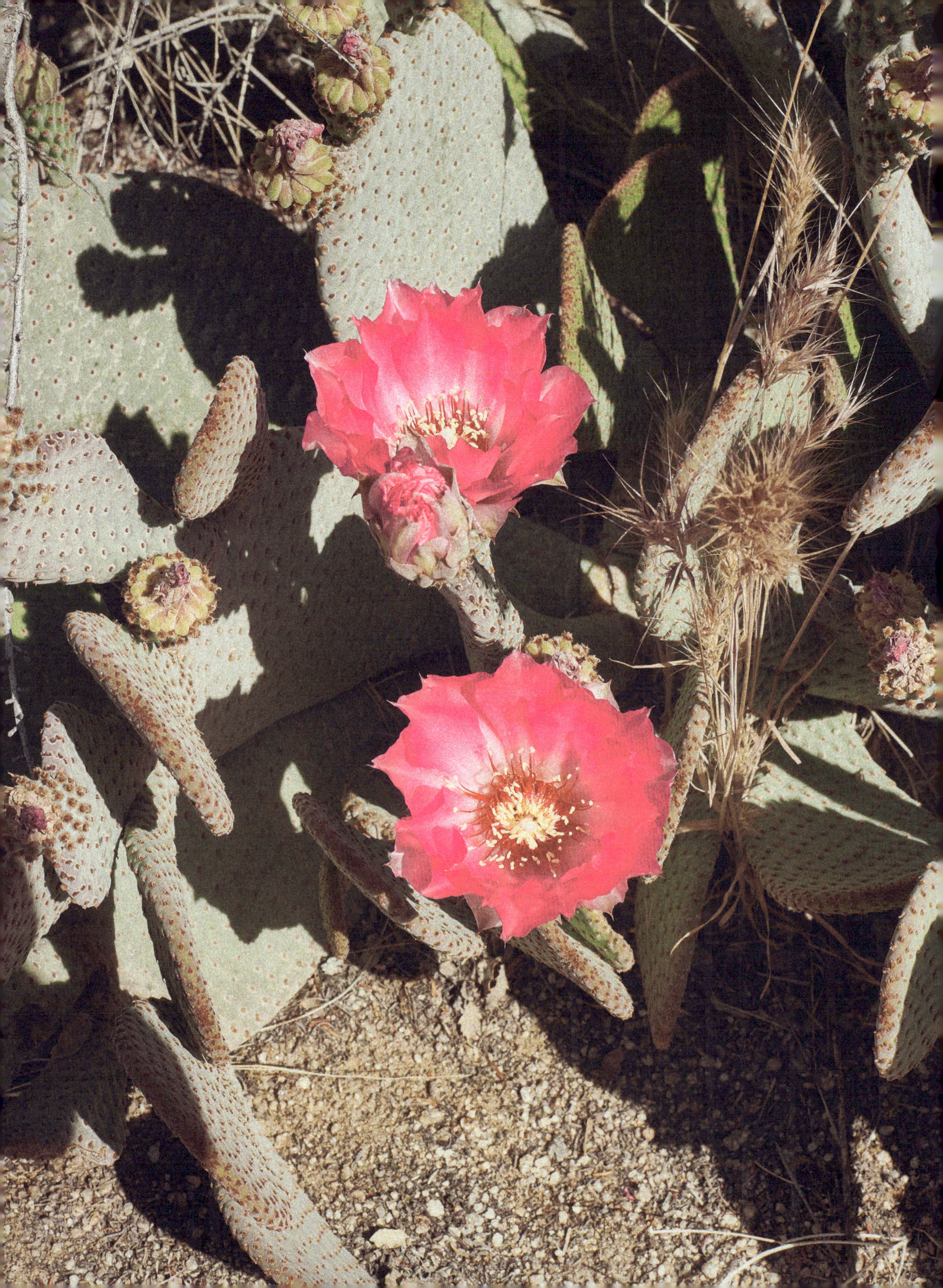

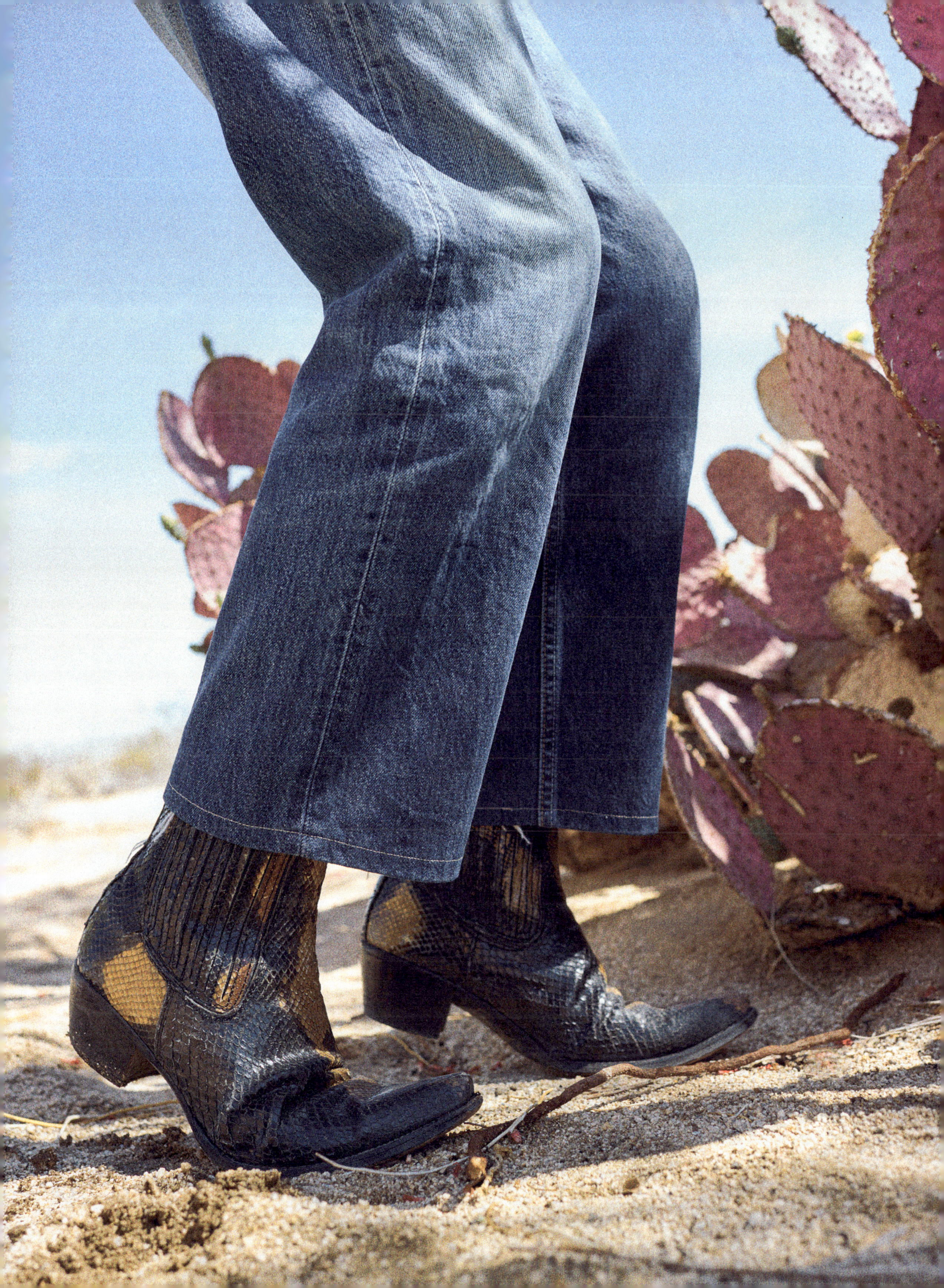

bunker into "a mecca for connectivity," enlisting his friends to teach dance styles including ballet, contemporary and jazz. "Where else can you go and have a great time with your friends as an adult that's not alcohol or nightlife based?" he asks. "When people come together to be truthful in the name of dance, joy and movement, it creates a different equation than we're used to in everyday life."

While teaching at the Sweat Spot, Heffington developed a new approach to working with nonprofessional dancers, using a vocabulary of images instead of ballet terminology to explain steps. "*Tendu, pas de bourrée, jeté* wouldn't get me anywhere. But when I asked people to bend over like they were an 80-year-old woman tying a shoelace, they could immediately understand what that movement looked like," he explains. Heffington now applies this technique to the film and TV projects he works on with actors with little prior movement experience, such as the homoerotic "I Need a Hero" dance scene performed by Austin Abrams in American teen drama *Euphoria*. "When I asked him to be like a mad scientist, and to put his hands above his head and shake them like he was changing the world, he got it."

The Sweat Spot's spirit has lived on in the community it forged, despite the studio having been demolished to make way for apartments. "It grew beyond the building itself. To this day people are still connected from that space," Heffington says. His classes also found new life online during COVID when he started Sweatfest, free weekly virtual dance sessions that became a lifeline for people around the globe. "For the first time, I really understood why the internet was created—to connect," he says. Not only did the classes give people hope and a reason to keep going, they also raised $300,000 for charities including Black Lives Matter, the American Civil Liberties Union and various queer organizations. "I'm always listening for 'downloads,'" says Heffington. "I never wanted to open a dance studio, but when people asked me, I realized it was a download and that I had to; I always follow my heart."

Heffington's latest download came to him in the desert town of Twentynine Palms, where he relocated at the beginning of the pandemic. "At first it was a safe haven, but then I was faced with the reality of being a middle-aged queer man in the middle of nowhere," he says. It wasn't until his neighbor, a real estate agent, invited him to see a unique property that he discovered his calling as a desert dweller. "As soon as I saw it, I said, *I'm opening a residency. This is what you do, Heffington, you create community, and you're going to do that out here. I'm going to infuse the desert with dance.*" Dancers won't be the only creatives invited to Heffington's residency—"I like the idea of a welder communicating with a poet, a chef and a roller skating artist"—and concrete output won't be expected from every visitor. "I want the space to be a place of respite where artists can swim, eat, be pampered and not think about work."

Heffington doesn't appear to be resting much himself, however: At the time of our interview, he's preparing to celebrate his 50th birthday and showing no signs of slowing down. He's hosted two events at the residency already, despite its seven structures still lacking doors and windows. "It's true Heffington style!" he says, laughing at his own impatience. "Friends from Oaxaca came up and we did traditional cooking, gave prayers and built a sweat lodge. We've also done performance events with poetry and drag to infuse the space with intention."

Looking to the future, Heffington dreams of choreographing for Broadway and is the resident DJ at Tits and Palms, his new desert-based party series for queer people and their allies. "My name is DJ Shovel," he grins, adding that, after years of having to cut his own music for shows, he's already pretty good. "I've fulfilled a niche market: I don't think a lot of people have ever experienced house music in the desert! I want to create a home for queerdom here."

Heffington has seemingly come full circle to where he started his dance journey: forging opportunities for expression in a secluded context. "I understand what it would be like for a queer person to grow up in this environment—I did it somewhere else," he says. Through all of the activities and projects he has planned, Heffington hopes that "the younger generation will be able to see people like themselves unabashedly living their best lives." It is exactly what Heffington has been doing, and encouraging others to do, ever since he first stepped foot in his local dance studio.

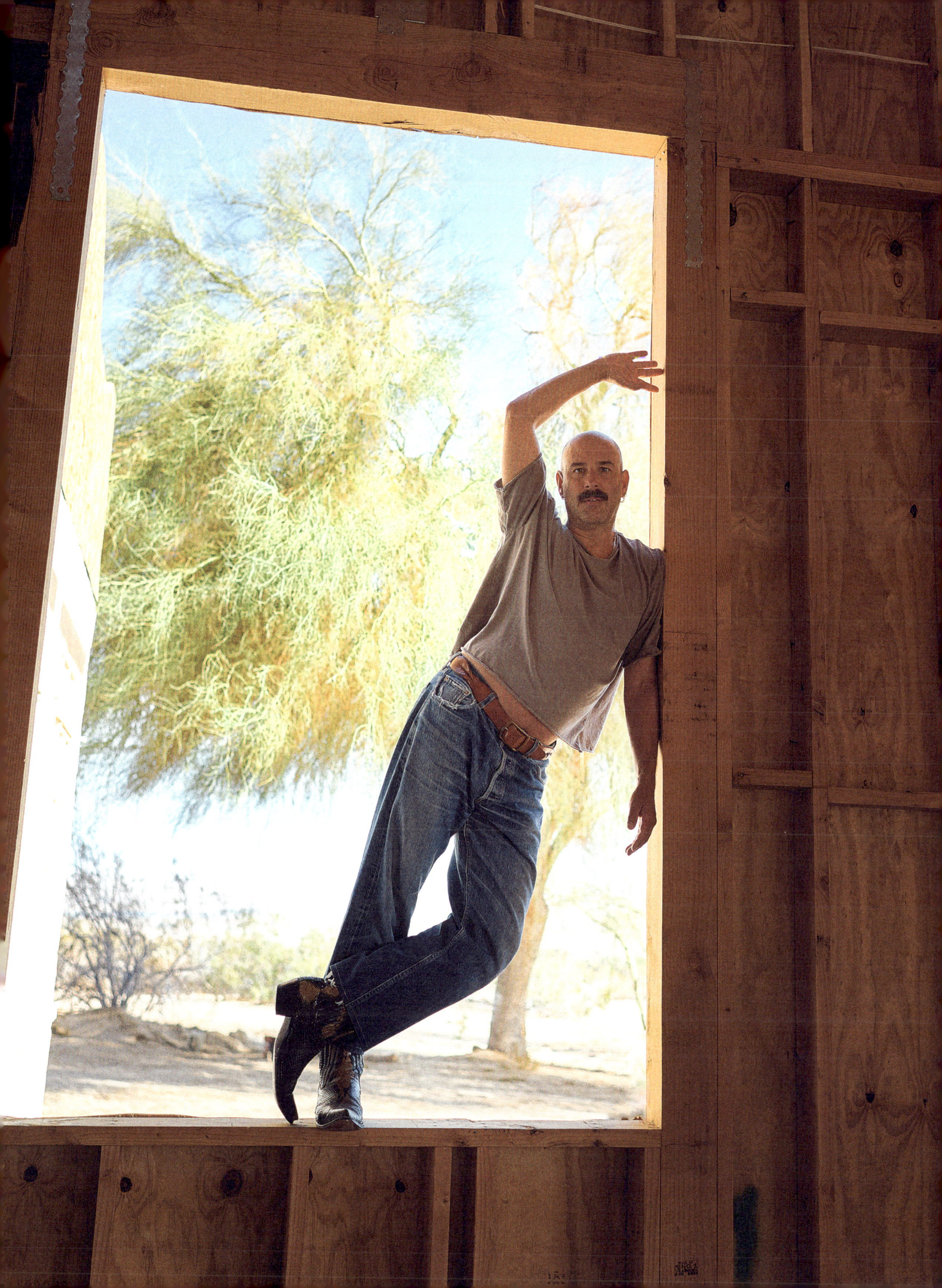

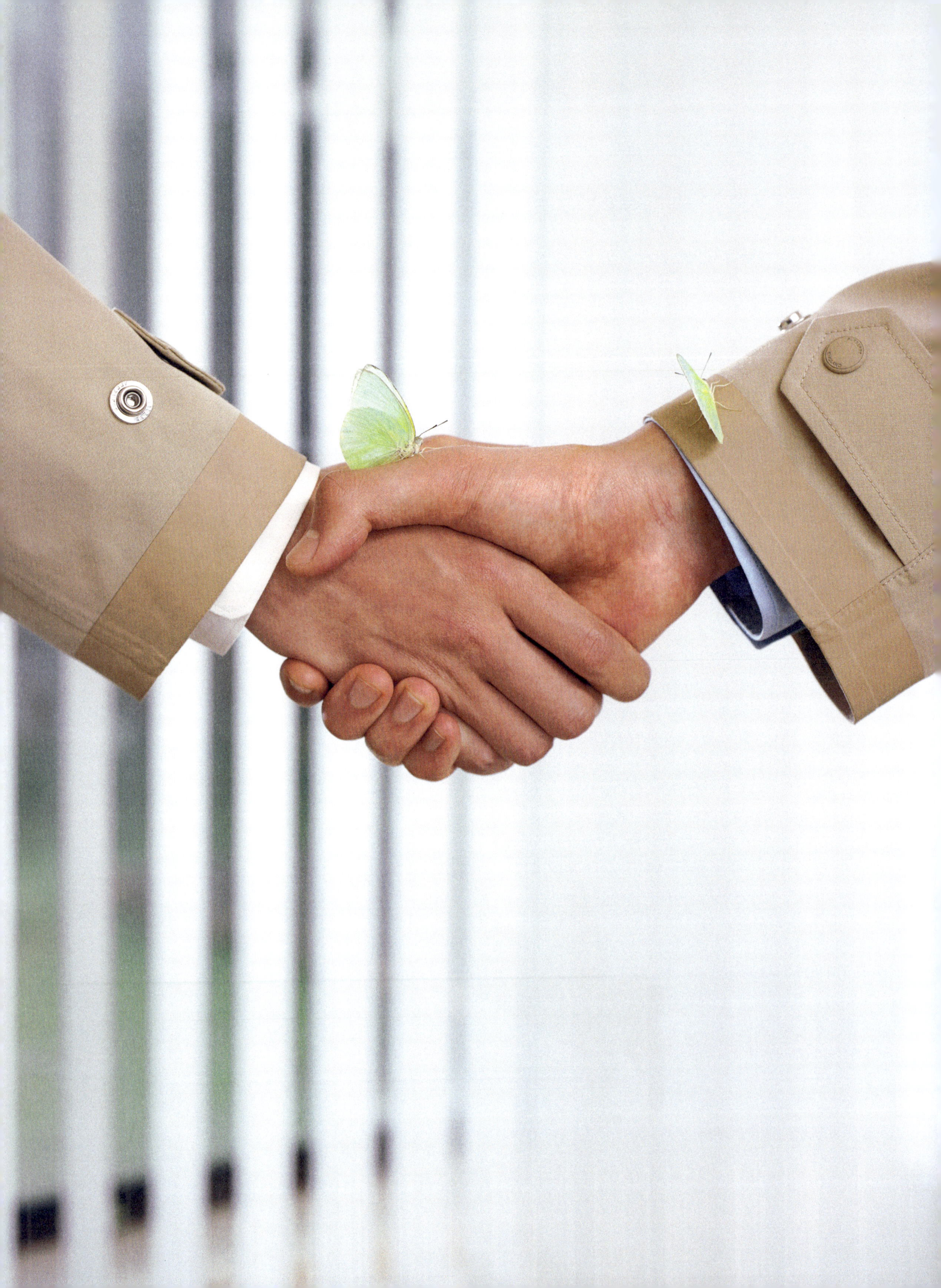

A fun lesson in
cultural faux pas.

105   A WORLD OF
            DIFFERENCE

            Photography
            XIAOPENG YUAN
            Styling
            ZINN ZHOU
            Words
            JOHN OVANS

SHOES OFF

Removing one's shoes is a deeply rooted tradition across many Asian and Middle Eastern cultures. Every visitor to a Japanese home, for example, will leave their shoes inside a *genkan*—a kind of porch with a raised border intended to prevent any negative ki (the equivalent of chi, or energy) from entering. The genkan also acts as a psychological gateway between the outside and inside worlds: As well as a mark of respect for the host, removing one's shoes is symbolic of leaving one's worries—as well as germs—at the door.

PERSONAL SPACE

The subconscious calculation we make as to how close we stand next to someone is known as "proxemics." It's a theory coined by cultural anthropologist Edward Hall in 1966 and suggests that the amount of distance people keep from one another is a consequence of where they grew up (apparently, everything from the wealth to the weather of a country factors into our perception of personal space). So-called "high contact" cultures usually emanate from warmer climes in South America, the Middle East and Southern Europe: A 2017 study found that Argentinians required the least personal space, while Romanians wanted the most.

(opposite)
Hua wears a cardigan and shirt by PRADA, shorts by DSQUARED2 and boots by BOTTEGA VENETA. Jiao wears an outfit by PRADA. Clogs by JW ANDERSON X WELLIPETS. Ballerina slippers by BALENCIAGA.

(right)
Jiao wears a sweater by SEAN SUEN, eyewear by GENTLE MONSTER and the stylist's own trousers. Hua wears a hoodie by LOEWE and shorts by DSQUARED2.

VOLUME LEVELS

In 2014, a pub in Ireland made global headlines for its "no bus or coach tours or loud Americans" policy. Theories abound as to what has created this enduring cultural stereotype; one suggestion proposes that since the US is so large, its residents simply have more air to fill. In Africa, Nigerians are singled out for the same crime, with local Twitterati proffering that it's necessary to make oneself heard above the millions of humming generators that power the country. Elsewhere, Germans are famously intolerant of noise in public spaces, to the extent that even the country's playgrounds are known to be comparatively quiet. It's no surprise, then, that it was the birthplace of the modern earplug in 1907.

(left)
Jiao wears a blazer, shorts and a tie by FERRAGAMO, a shirt by BURBERRY and eyewear by GENTLE MONSTER. Hua wears a tie by BURBERRY and the stylist's own shirt.

(opposite)
Hua wears a trench coat and tank top by BALENCIAGA and eyewear by GENTLE MONSTER.

TIPPING CULTURE

Much to the chagrin of many foreigners, who believe employers should just raise staff wages, tipping culture in the US is well-established and customers are expected to add 20% or more to the final bill. It has been argued that tipping is a legacy of slavery, and that it first appeared in the 1850s after upwardly mobile Americans sought to mimic the tradition of masters offering service staff extra cash for good service. Following the abolition, many previously enslaved people took up work as waiters, barbers, porters and servants, but employers continued not to pay them, requesting that guests offered a tip instead to circumvent the new constitution.

PUNCTUALITY

In many countries, time is a mere suggestion rather than a stipulation. Across the Islamic world, for example, attempts to wrestle a solid commitment out of someone may be met with the word "inshallah." In other words, you'll meet on time if God wills it. Although Islam, in fact, places importance on punctuality, reflected in the strict ritual of daily prayers, culturally speaking, inshallah permits people to live in the moment—to be waylaid by the unexpected, even if it means turning up hours late, or perhaps even not at all.

(opposite)
Hua wears a trench coat by BURBERRY, a shirt by GUCCI and eyewear by GENTLE MONSTER with the stylist's own skirt, shoes and socks. Jiao wears a jacket and shirt by BURBERRY, a tie by FERRAGAMO, eyewear by GENTLE MONSTER and the stylist's own trousers and shoes.

(right)
Hua wears a tank top by JW ANDERSON, shorts by XIMONLEE and shoes by JW ANDERSON X WELLIPETS. Jiao wears a coat, vest, tie and boots by BOTTEGA VENETA, a shirt by BURBERRY, shorts by DSQUARED2 and eyewear by GENTLE MONSTER.

(overleaf)
Hua and Jiao wear outfits by XANDER ZHOU.

Makeup: Freya Ni. Hair: Fuzai at HairPro Studio. Models: Hengxin Hua & Tong Jiao at LongTeng Management. Producer: Xinzhi Huang.

SMART CASUAL

A business trip to Japan or Korea will most likely involve the occupational hazard of hangovers, as both are countries where business and booze are inextricably linked. *Hoesik* is a Korean word meaning "dinner with coworkers"—a euphemism, essentially, for seeing what a bottle of soju reveals about your colleague's true personality. In Seoul, Mondays are such a big night for hoesik that the city's roads are often less busy with traffic. Hierarchy is everything, even when blind drunk: drinking your shot before your boss has one poured is frowned upon.

KINFOLK

KIRAI-BASHI
While in southern parts of China, it's commonplace for people to wash their own chopsticks in a bowl of boiled water before eating, it's not the same elsewhere across the country. In fact, a host might be aghast at the suggestion their cutlery was unclean. In Japan, chopstick etiquette is known as *kirai-bashi*, which loosely translates as "displeasing chopsticks." In both cultures, there are myriad rules and associated superstitions: never use them to point at people, for example, or leave them sticking upwards in rice as this resembles the incense sticks offered to deceased family members.

Part 3.
SCANDINAVIA
Conversations with the region's leading lights.
114 — 176

114	Urban Doom
126	Amalie Smith
134	Tove Lo
146	Karin Mamma Andersson
158	Fares Fares
166	Ruben Östlund

(Fashion)

A saturnine mélange of subversive styles.

URBAN DOOM

PHOTOGRAPHY ZHONG LIN
STYLING CHEN YU

(above) Asher wears a top and trousers by MUGLER X H&M.
(previous) Dan wears an earring by MUGLER X H&M.

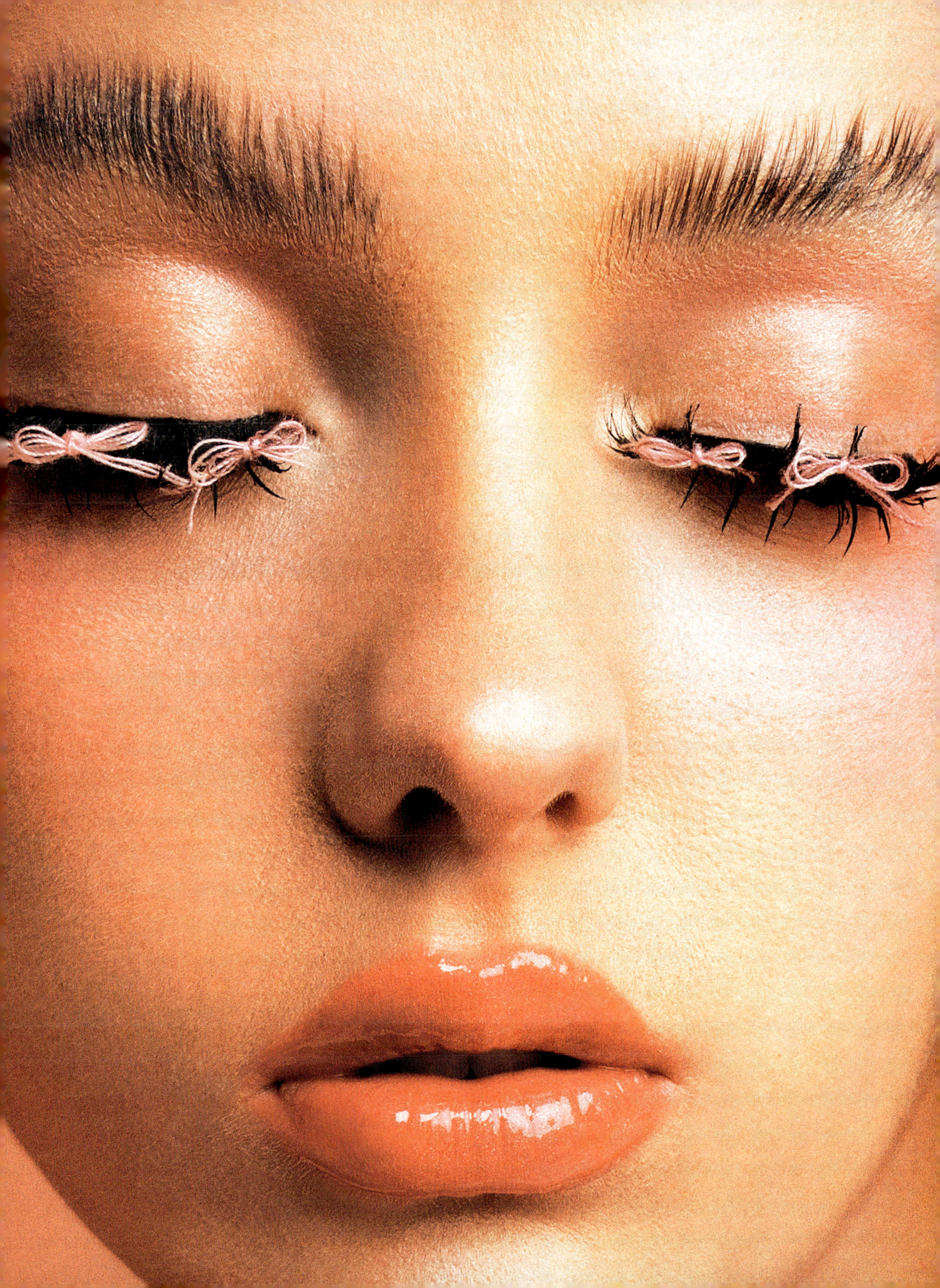

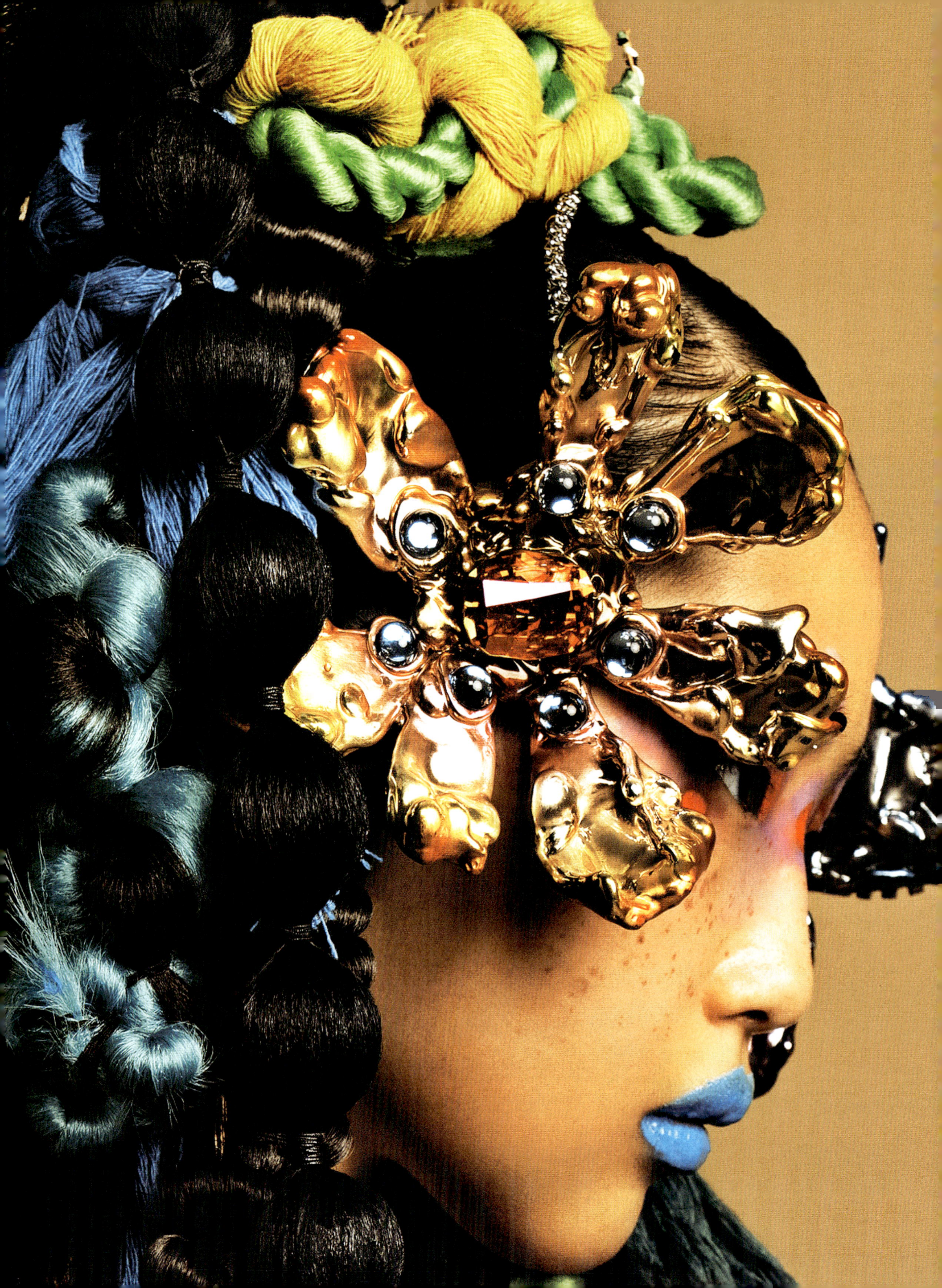

(below)   Wahcee wears a top and shoes by MOTOGUO.
(opposite) Peng wears a headpiece by MELTED POTATO.

KINFOLK

119

(below)　　Dan wears an earring by MUGLER X H&M and a necklace by LOUIS VUITTON.
(opposite)　Sofi wears shoes by MIU MIU.

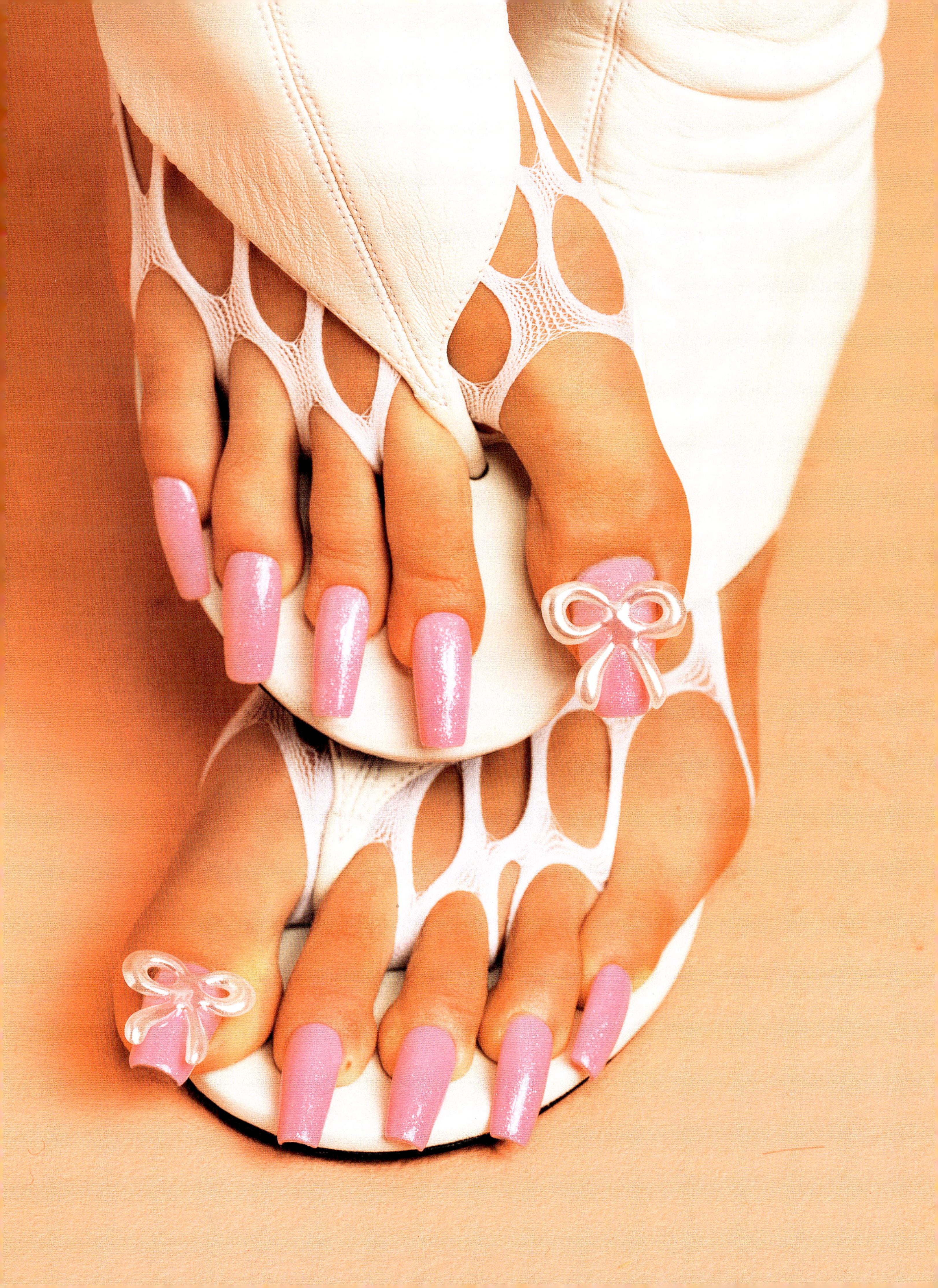

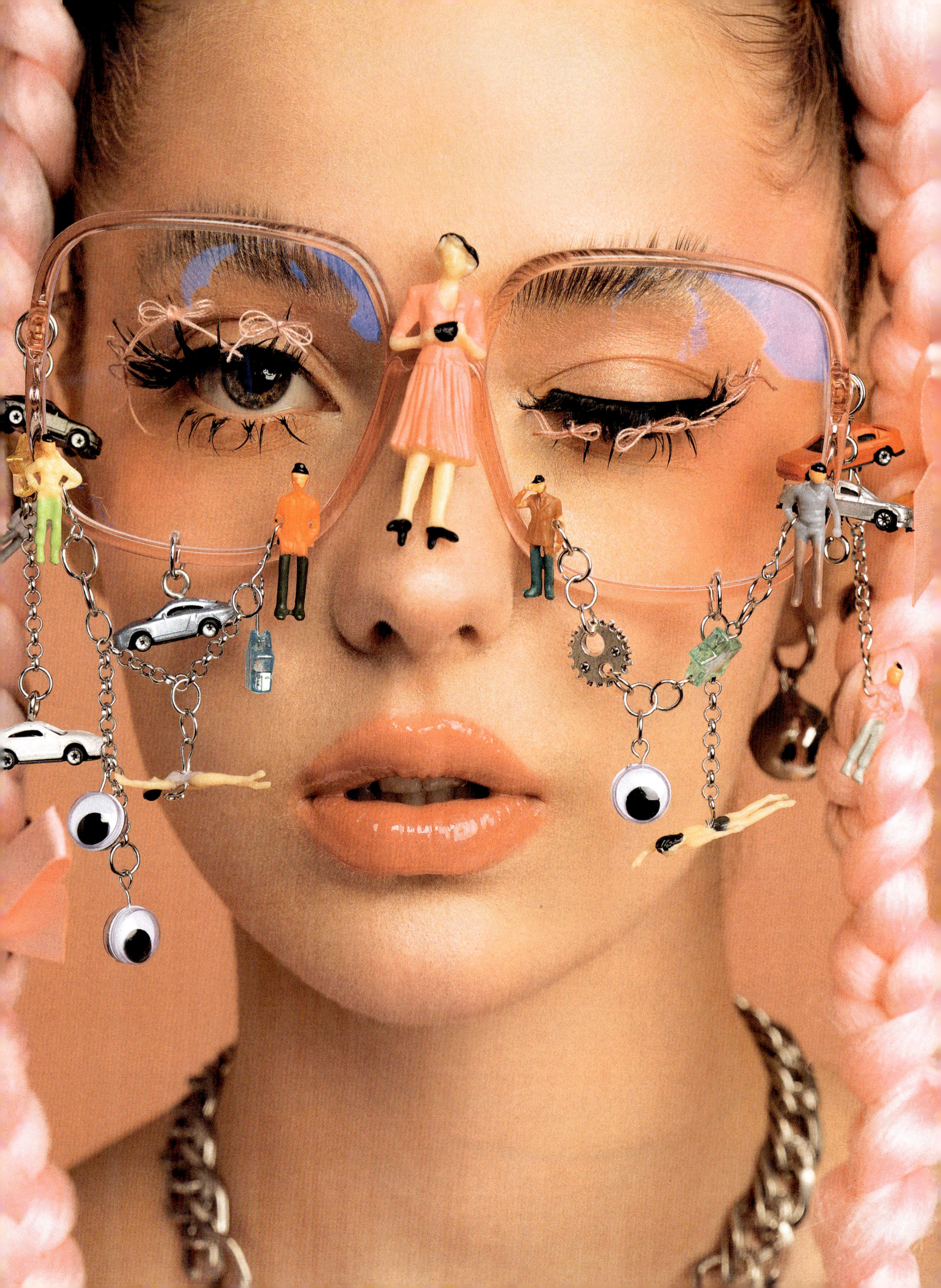

(opposite)   Sofi wears earrings by MOTOGUO and a necklace by MELTED POTATO.

(above) Wahcee wears shoes by MOTOGUO.
(opposite) Peng wears a headpiece and ring by MELTED POTATO.

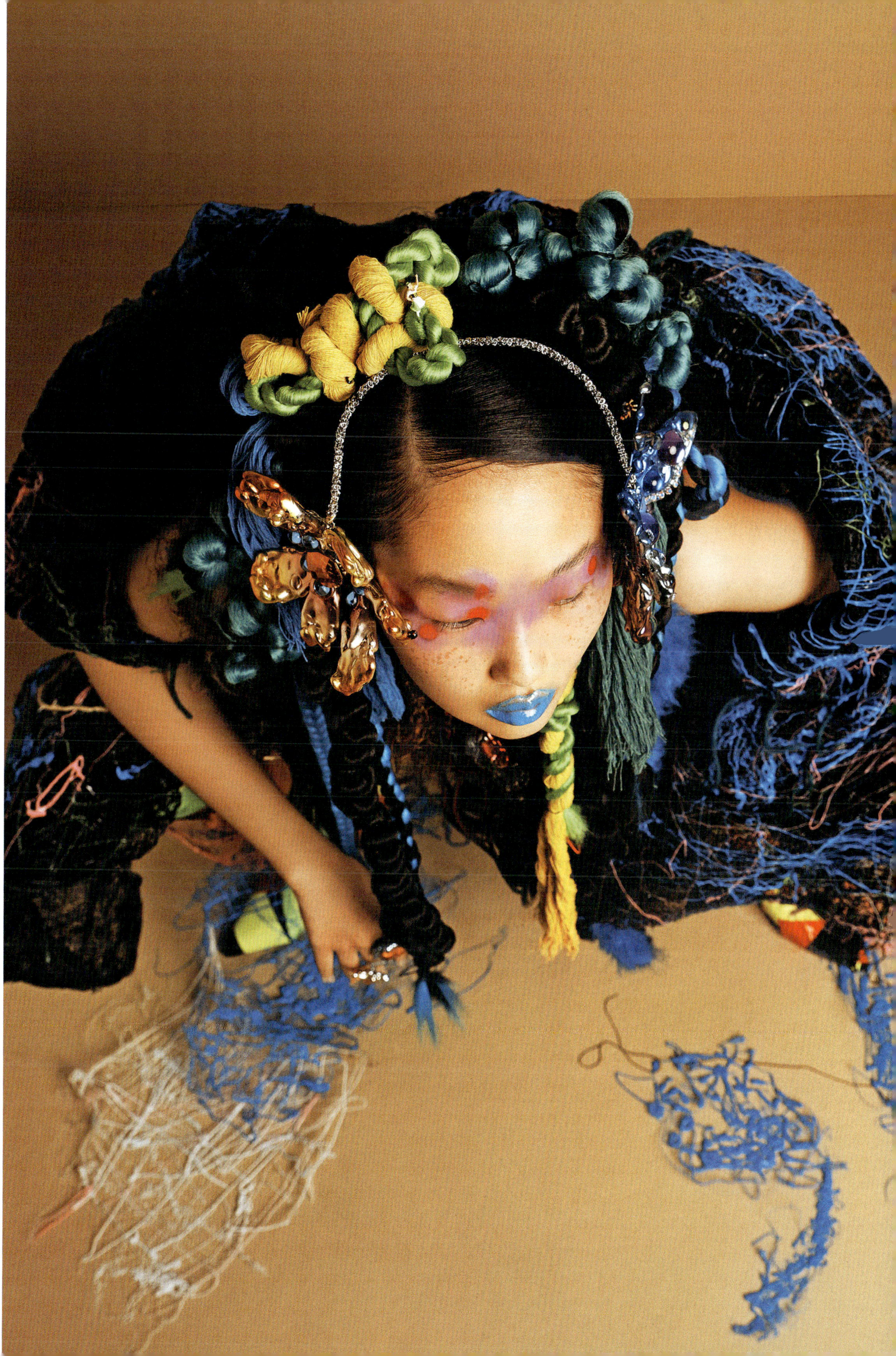

The Danish arts writer finding clarity between the lines.

Amalie SMITH

(The Writer)

WORDS BENJAMIN DANE
PHOTOGRAPHY CECILIE JEGSEN
STYLING SIMONE HENNEBERG

SCANDINAVIA

Amalie Smith's most recent novel, *Thread Ripper*, presents itself as a "hybrid." Two different narrative threads—one printed on the left pages and one printed on the facing right pages—decipher the connections between old weaving looms and computers, all the while merging accounts of iconic women in science and mythology together with philosophical and personal ruminations into one coherent story. The term "hybrid" is meant as a genre, but it would also be a fitting way to describe the entire body of work of the Danish writer and artist.

At the age of 37, Smith has published eight books and had exhibitions from Malmö to Melbourne, displaying eclectic artworks—sculpture, sound and video installations. She has won several prizes since graduating from the Danish Academy of Creative Writing in 2009 (and from the Royal Danish Academy of Fine Arts in 2015) for her curious, experimental writing and artworks that address subjects ranging from traditional Greek dancing to carnivorous plants on the small Danish island of Læsø. Each project delves ever deeper into Smith's fundamental interest in how idea and matter are intertwined. Ultimately, it's all about Smith making sense of the world for herself, she says when we meet at a café in her neighborhood of Nørrebro in Copenhagen.

BENJAMIN DANE: Your latest novel, *Thread Ripper*, was published in English last year. Can you tell me about the concept?

AMALIE SMITH: A few years ago, I did my first large-scale commission for a high school here in Copenhagen, consisting of three large digitally woven tapestries. In the process, I became increasingly intrigued by how weaving and computer technology are connected. The first computers used punch cards, originally invented for industrial weaving machines. These computers were as big as a house, and people would program them by plugging in and removing wires.

Today, we often talk about the digital as something immaterial, completely disconnected from the physical world, but sometimes I think we need to remind ourselves that it all exists in large server racks somewhere. It has materiality. And when you trace the computer all the way back to the loom, suddenly there's a 7,000-year history. The computer didn't just emerge out of nothing; it has undergone a physical transformation, and I was excited to challenge the notion of the disembodied, virtual world, connecting it to something tangible that one can touch and feel.

Then, I came up with the idea of having two separate narrative threads—one consisting mostly of notes and reflections and one that's more story-driven—that weave together throughout the book. It might sound a bit esoteric, but it actually makes sense when you read it. I always try to think equally about the form and content of my work, and when the two really come together, that's when it becomes exciting for me.

BD: What does your daily writing process look like?

AS: It's kind of chaotic, to be honest. I'm not the kind of writer who can sit down at my desk every day from nine to five and just type it out. In many ways,

"I never try to mystify anything."

I wish I could. I don't always write daily, and sometimes months go by without me putting a single word on paper, which is a shame because it takes time to get back into the flow. But when you have a dual practice like I do, you're constantly juggling multiple balls, always thinking, organizing, responding, generating new ideas, seeking funding. When I do find time to write, it always begins with something that already exists—never a blank page—whether it's a line of thought from a previous project or perhaps a theory that has caught my attention.

BD: Do you have a specific reader in mind when you write?

AS: Most of the time, I think I'm writing for myself—trying to understand and organize the world. I write the sort of books that I would find exciting to read. Also, I've been really privileged to be able to live off my writing and art for the last 10 years or so without having to think too much about necessarily writing a bestseller. We have a great grant system in Denmark and a strong public support for the arts, which has enabled me to experiment, follow my intuition and write my books in the way they "wanted" to be written. If a publisher just wanted to make a bestseller, it probably wouldn't be good advice to do two narrative threads like I did with *Thread Ripper*—but maybe it's good for the work of art, and luckily, it's been quite well-received too.

BD: You've described your work as having "hybrid energy." What does that term mean to you?

AS: There are so many things—both in science and in the rest of the world—that are not purely one thing or another, but rather intermediate forms and composite matters. One of my books was reviewed in a Danish newspaper,

(opposite)   Smith wears a shirt and boots by MARK KENLY DOMINO TAN and a skirt by SLOTH ROUSING.
(previous)   She wears an outfit by AERON and shoes by BILLI BI.
(overleaf)   She wears an outfit by BIRROT and the stylist's own shoes.

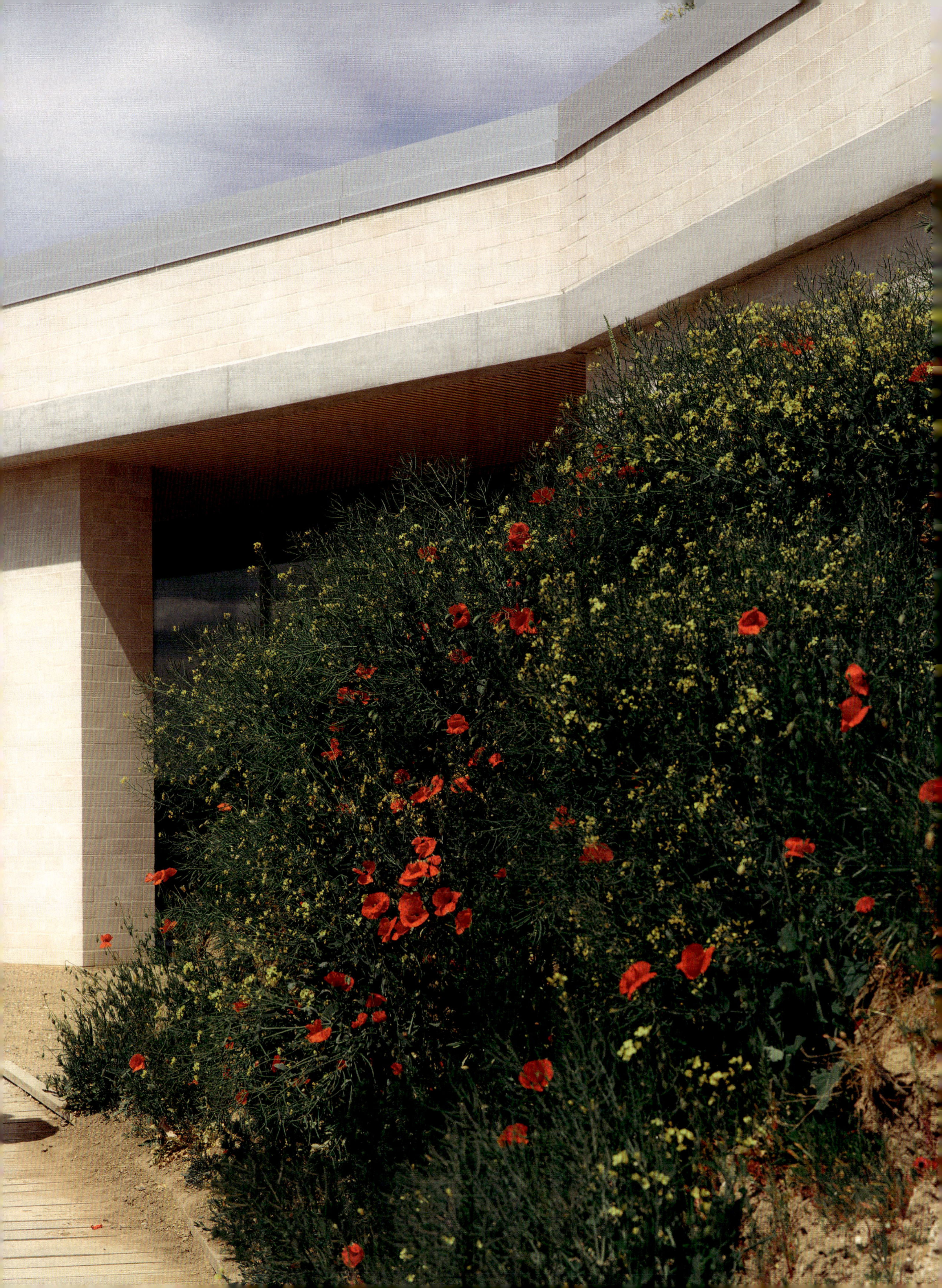

Location: Stevns Klint Experience

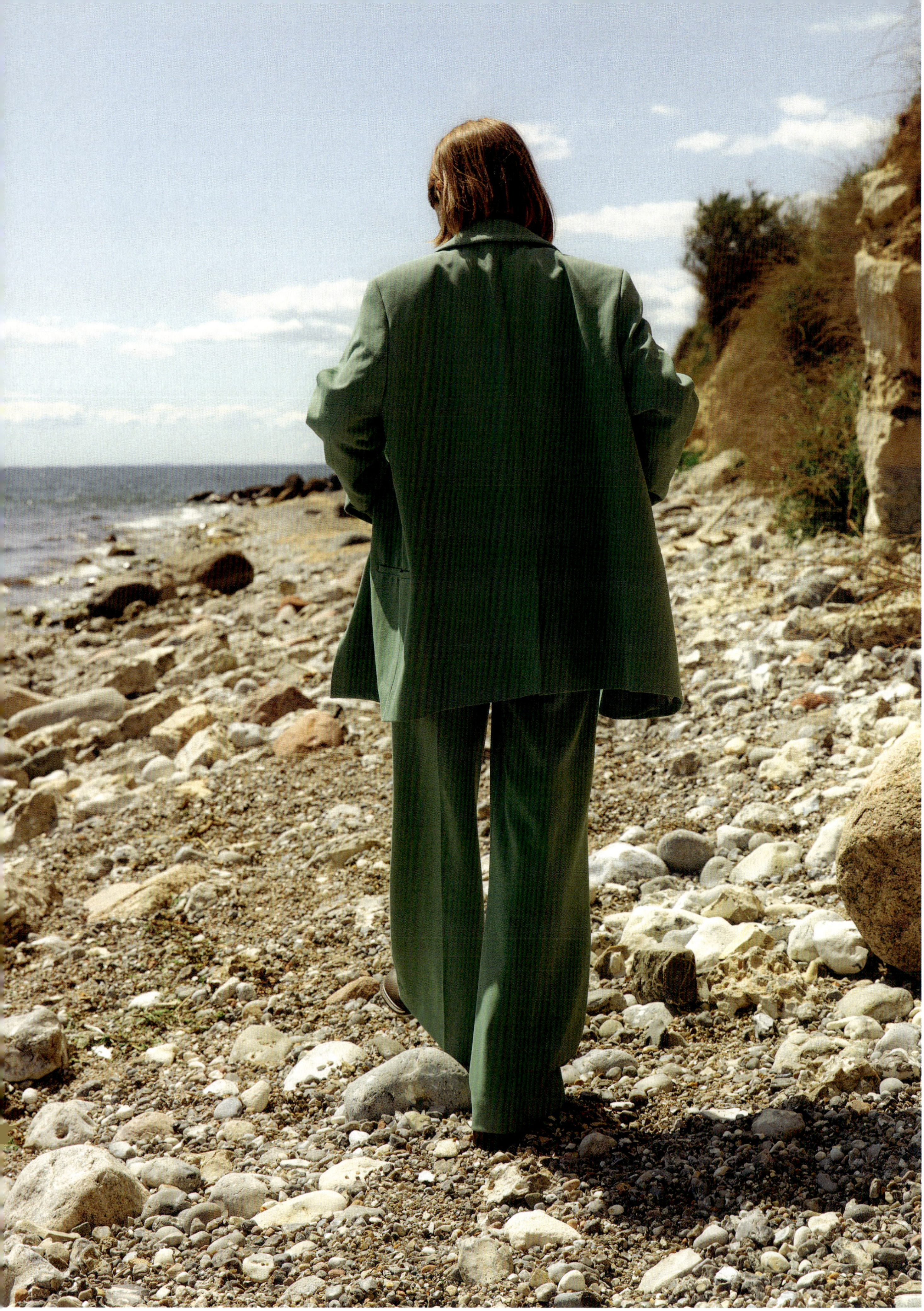

(opposite) Smith wears an outfit by LOVECHILD 1979 and shoes by MARK KENLY DOMINO TAN.

where the critic wrote that my book wasn't incoherent per se, but more a Frankenstein-like, pieced-together entity, and he was missing something a little more definitive and complete.[1] But I want to make a case for the hybrid, because I believe the world is one. I've always been drawn toward hybrid subjects, the ones where you need to draw from various disciplines to fully understand the field you're entering.

BD: You often deal with quite complex subjects. To what extent are you concerned with making your work accessible?

AS: I really try to write in a way that I believe everyone can understand. Of course, that doesn't mean it's for everyone, but I never try to mystify anything. I try to arrange the elements within the subject matter I delve into and juxtapose them in a way where they start to make some kind of sense for me, and hopefully also for the reader. Maybe it's fine that some parts of literature exist in a closed bubble—most of us also don't understand everything going on in molecular biology, and that's okay; not everyone needs to understand everything. But I hope and think that my work exists on the border.

BD: How do you view your role as a writer and artist in a broader sense? Is there some sort of higher purpose to it, besides you making sense of the world?

AS: I believe that there's a huge task ahead for both literature and the visual arts that revolves around the mental shift needed to even come close to the transition that climate change demands of our society. Often, the public discourse is about technological quick fixes enabling us to continue living as we always have, but I believe that we need to think about humanity and nature in a fundamentally different way. We have imagined that the Earth has infinite resources, even though everyone can see that it doesn't. We have imagined ourselves as an entity separated from nature, but that is completely absurd considering how intertwined we are with its ecosystem: the bacteria we have in our stomachs, the way our bodies are built to withstand gravitational force.

In the arts, we have so many years of work that speaks to humans as independent individuals who can realize themselves at the expense of nature and other people, and there is a need to rewrite that. It took centuries to arrive here, and it will take not just one book to turn the narrative around and save the world; it must be written anew—over and over—by many different people, in many different ways.

BD: How do you see a novel like *Thread Ripper* in that context?

AS: When I talk about the materiality of the digital, it's an attempt to anchor it in the world—anchor it in nature. *Thread Ripper* is very much about trying to understand the world in a different way.

"When I write, it always begins with something that already exists—never a blank page."

(1) The *Politiken* review of *Thread Ripper* was largely positive, with the critic Lilian Munk Rösing giving the book six stars and calling it "a formidable book." "Everything is beautifully intertwined," she wrote.

KINFOLK

133

TOVE

WORDS	TARA JOSHI
PHOTOGRAPHY	EMMAN MONTALVAN
STYLING	ANNIE & HANNAH

(The Musician)

The radically honest singer-songwriter on the big feelings behind her biggest hits.

LO

THE POP STAR RISING

HIGHER AND HIGHER.

When Ebba Tove Elsa Nilsson was 15 years old, she won a prize for a short story she wrote. In it, two best friends have grown apart because one of them gets a boyfriend; in response, the other friend starts stalking her, and ends up killing her "just to keep her close." Nilsson—known professionally as pleasure-seeking pop star Tove Lo—is laughing as she recounts this tale. "It was pretty dark," she concedes, "but there was humor to it. And Sweden being Sweden, they were like, '*Yay!*' Most of the stories I wrote were about a girl doing twisted things."

Since Nilsson broke through 10 years ago with the sleeper hit "Habits (Stay High)," songs with undercurrents of deviance and discomfort—about girls doing "twisted" things—have become something of a mainstay in her oeuvre. There's a reason, after all, that the 35-year-old singer-songwriter has carried the label of the "saddest girl in Sweden" for so long; her music has largely explored the murkiness of hedonism—the joys and exuberance, the escape and the sensuality, but also its more concerning and painful underbelly.

Before "Habits" gained internet virality and propelled her to stardom in her own right, Nilsson's music career started with writing songs for other artists, something she still does to this day (she has writing credits for Dua Lipa, Charlie XCX, Lorde and more). But there is a distinct personality that comes through in the songs that she writes for herself: propulsive, breathy, druggy, wry, a little depraved. These are lyrics predominantly rooted in some form of reality for the artist; not so much a considered, manufactured party-girl persona, she explains, but an insight into some of her real thoughts and experiences, albeit ones that are sometimes exaggerated and wrought larger than life.

Though she was signed to a major label for her first four albums, Nilsson was careful to retain autonomy over her image and style. "I found it really hard to describe myself when I was starting out," she says. "The first album, I felt like I had no idea how to say what I was like, but I remember having this feeling that I didn't want to get pushed in the direction people wanted to put me in visually just to try and keep it commercial, so I pushed a lot more toward the left."

Nilsson is thoughtful like this throughout our interview, and also pretty ebullient. She's on tour, so she's speaking to me on the phone from Orlando ("We're staying in the Disney World area so it's very surreal; everything here is like a fantasyland!"). Back on her second and third albums, 2016's *Lady Wood* and 2017's *Blue Lips*, she says, she was not in a good place: "I guess I was just like, *I can't put on a brave face, I just want to be how I am and live in these feelings.* I just wanted to show where I was at in life." In the short films that she made to accompany the records, she pushed into the "left" again, establishing her artistic realm as a lusty, seedy world of late

(previous)   Nilsson wears a top and skirt by MELITTA BAUMEISTER, a shirt by MARC JACOBS, boots by MAISON MARTIN MARGIELA, a ring by J. HANNAH and the stylist's own earrings.
(opposite)   She wears a dress by MELITTA BAUMEISTER and earrings by PANCONESI.

nights, parties, friendships and lovers. "I can barely look at those [short films] now," she reflects. "I'm so proud of them—I think they're so beautiful—but it's hard for me to watch and know how dark of a time that was for me."

Of course, these days, life looks a little different for the artist than it did back in her 20s: She's now based in LA and married to the creative director Charlie Twaddle. "I've been in a really good place now for many years," she says, matter-of-factly. It's not that getting older and—to her own surprise—having a spouse, means her lifestyle has completely changed. In her 2022 music video for the club banger "2 Die 4," she walks around rocky terrain wearing a gold corset and a matching strap-on dildo: Clearly, Nilsson still likes to have fun. Acts like this are also a welcome fuck-you to the male journalists who, for years, she recalls asking questions, like "Don't you ever worry that no one's going to want to be with a girl like you forever when you're such a whore?" (Thankfully, she says, it's clear in more recent years that many of them have learned that those questions are totally unacceptable.)

> " If I'm in a dark place now, I don't use partying to cope. I try to stay in the feelings and work it out."

Nilsson, her friends and her husband all still party, and she doesn't see that changing anytime soon, but now, she explains, it feels more intentional and respectful—both when it comes to others and herself. "If I'm in a dark place now, I don't use partying to cope," she says. "I try to stay in the feelings and work it out. And so now partying and doing wild things are things I do when I'm feeling good and I want to enhance the feeling and have a good time." She stands by the necessity of going out to shake it off when things are a bit shitty but is now more conscious of her boundaries. "If you're constantly running from it and constantly trying to numb your feelings…," she pauses, "I don't do that anymore. That's where I feel like it got destructive." Even looking back at "Habits"—a song that was broadly about partying excessively to try to forget about someone—is no longer a testament to pain. "That song changed my life," she explains, "so it's not sad for me anymore. Now it's nostalgic and euphoric."

(opposite) Nilsson wears a coat by WE11DONE, shoes by MAISON MARTIN MARGIELA, rings by J. HANNAH, an ear cuff by FARIS, vintage socks, her own earrings and the stylist's own necklace.

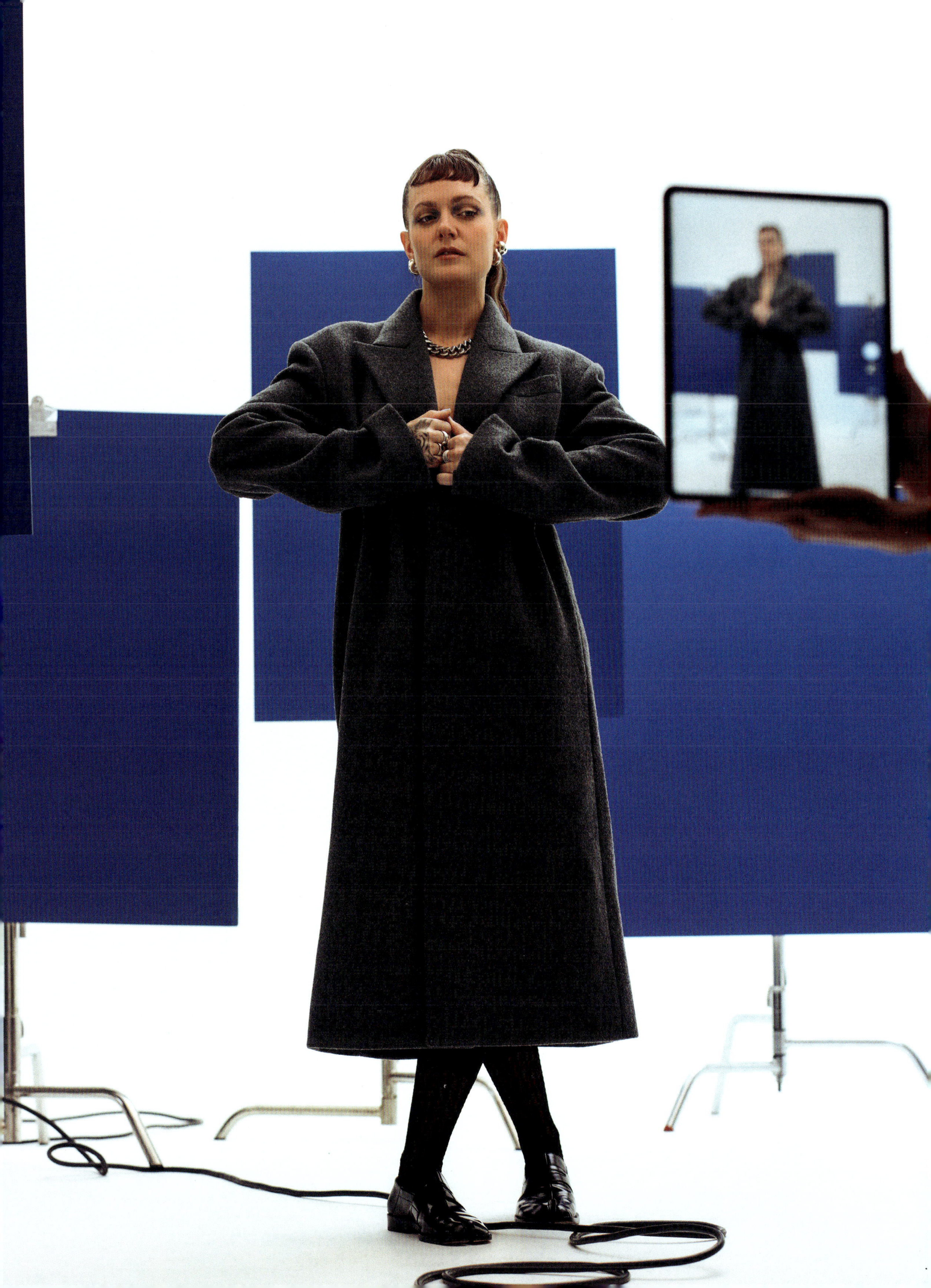

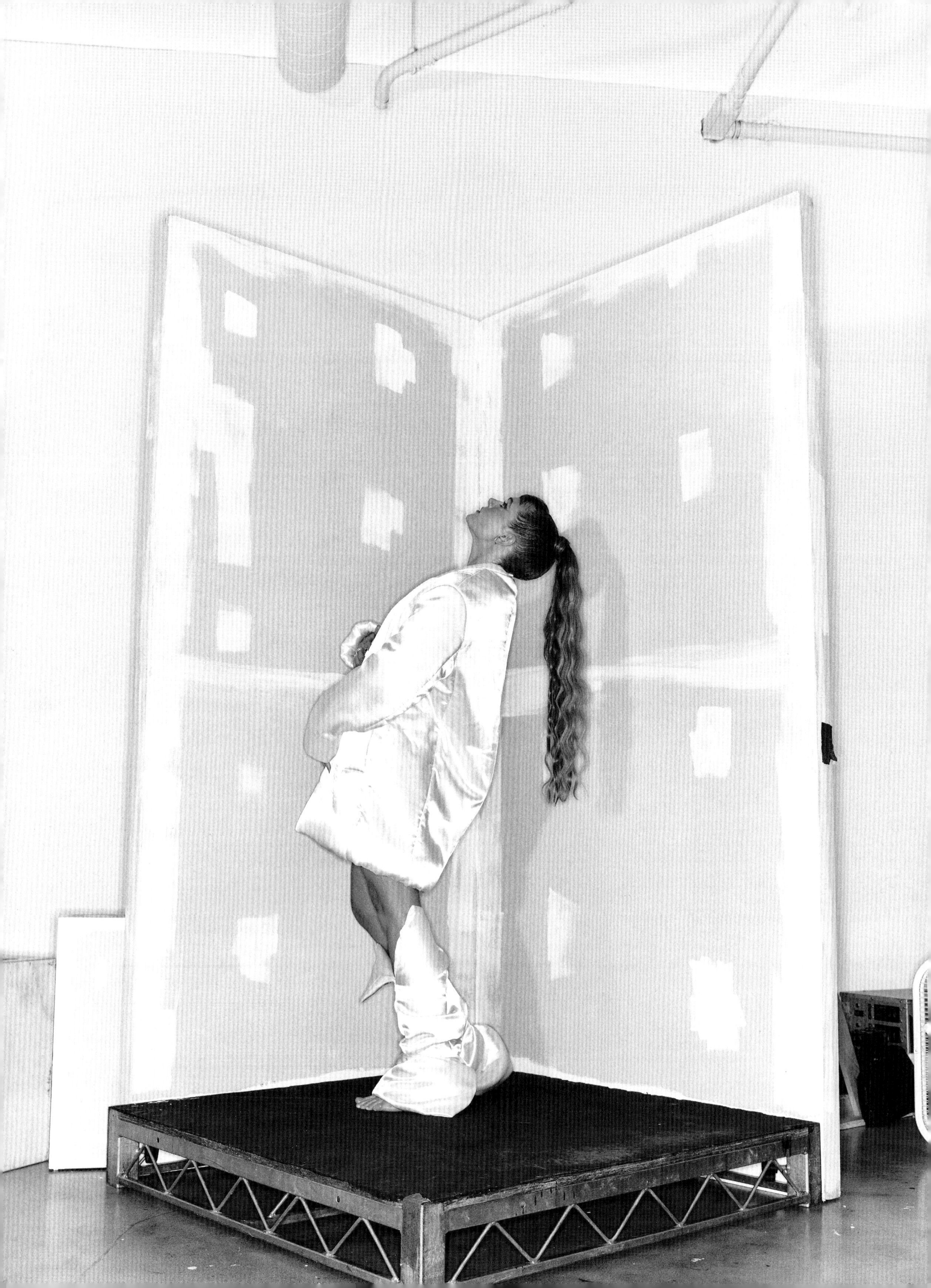

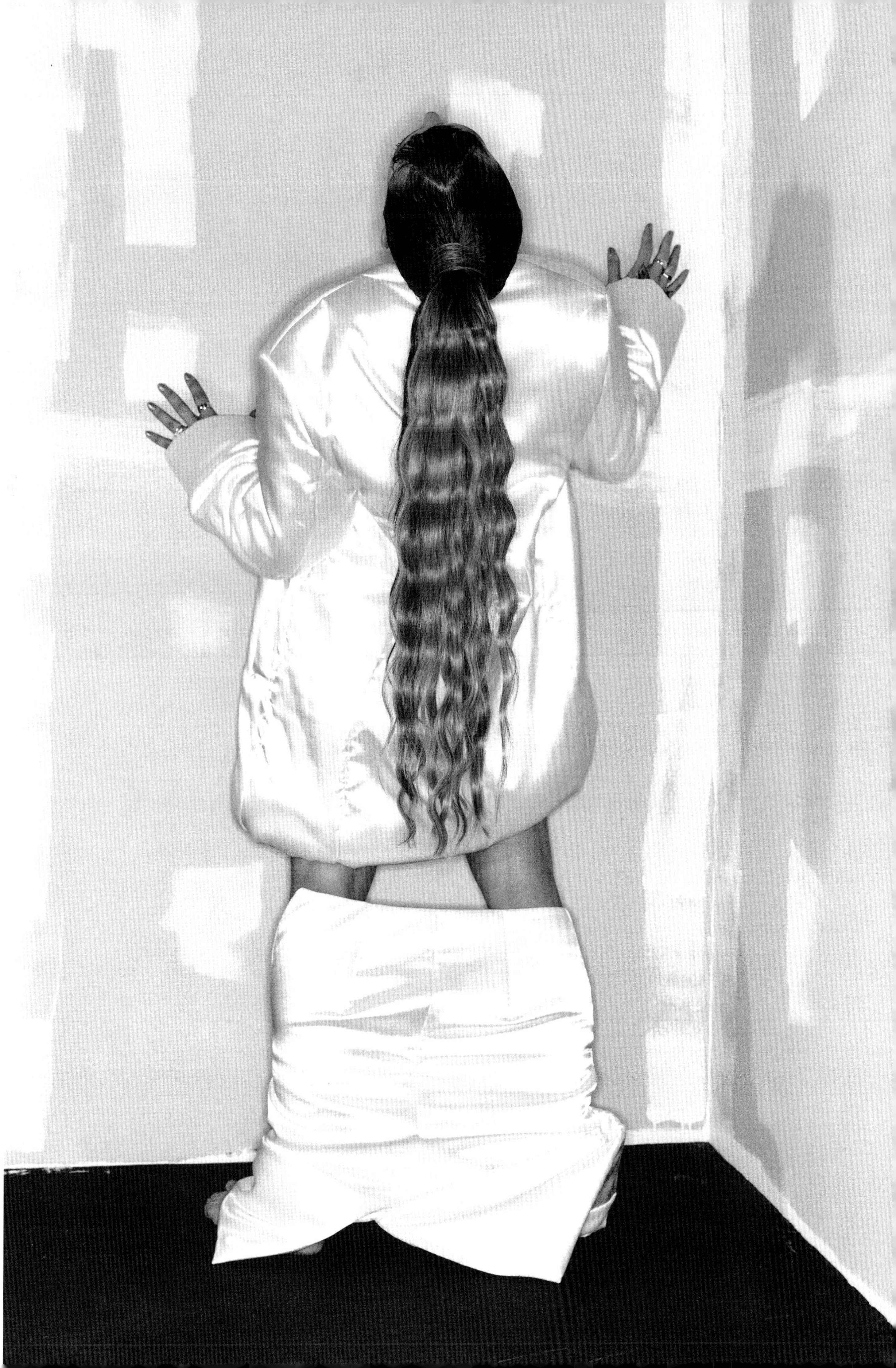

I put it to her that the "saddest girl in Sweden" label might now feel at odds with where she is these days, both geographically and emotionally. "It was something I wore like a badge of honor," she says, before hesitating. "But if I could pick one sentence to describe me as an artist, that would not be it anymore. Or ever, to be honest: I was vulnerable through and through, but that doesn't always mean sadness. I'm happy a lot of the time, I'm sad a lot of the time too. No artist or human is just one thing. We're all contradictory in the big spectrum of views and feelings."

Certainly, the breadth of the spectrum is explored on her latest album, 2022's *Dirt Femme*, a gleaming dance record which finds Nilsson disarmingly raw in new ways: on the track "Suburbia," for example, where she offers lines like "So if we had a baby / You'd love that more than me?" and on "Grapefruit," a seemingly euphoric bop that's actually about her teenage bulimia. Still, the theme that runs the gamut of her work remains true: her stark honesty. "I think maybe the way I express myself, for some people, is like, *Oh, why would you admit to that feeling? That's not something you talk about out loud!*" she laughs.

A year on from the release of *Dirt Femme*, she remains immensely proud of the record: It's her first launch on Pretty Swede Records, her own label. "Going independent is obviously a lot more work, but so far I've loved it," she says. She admits, however, that tracks like "Grapefruit" are not always easy to revisit. She was concerned about "laying out all the cards" when recording it, given how triggering and emotional it had the potential to be. She was also worried that an illness she had already worked through could become what defined her from that point. But she says she felt a calling to "keep following your instinct and not edit yourself; write what you need to write."

(above)   Nilsson wears a jacket, trousers and boots by HERMÈS, a shirt by COPERNI, earrings by ACNE STUDIOS, rings by J. HANNAH and the stylist's own tie.

Even so, repeatedly having to return to the song when she performs it live is complicated, she says. "It varies so much night by night," she explains. "I get really bad PMS, like, every two months, and I get this really bad feeling. I *know* it's not how I feel, but I cannot shake the feeling. I feel really insecure: I start to dissect my face and my body, my voice, how I move, spending four or five days in this little cocoon of hate for myself. And I keep this mantra: *This will pass, this will pass*. But if I perform that song during those days, it's not cathartic—it's just really hard." On those days when she wishes she didn't have to revisit the sentiments of the song onstage, she looks to the audience for strength. "I find the people in the crowd who I can tell the song means a lot to and I just look at them and think, *I'm doing this for this person*," she says and starts laughing. "And that helps me to not just start crying onstage."

> "I was vulnerable through and through, but that doesn't always mean sadness."

Perhaps that interplay between battling with her brain and finding contentment is why the candor in her lyrics—be it those more difficult tracks about her insecurities and pain, or the frank and delicious lines about her nipples being hard or giddily guiding her partner to give her oral sex—all feels very raw and real. It's something that she attributes to her upbringing in the Skåne region of southern Sweden. "It's funny, because I feel this contradiction in my childhood," she says. Her mother is a therapist and her father cofounded a successful fintech company, and she recalls that the area they lived in, which was quite affluent, could feel judgmental—like no one was showing their flaws. "Everyone kept their face on all the time." At home, however, her family talked about everything: "We would express how we felt a lot. Me and my dad would fight when I was a teenager, but he was always good at apologizing. He has a lot of authority, but he's a very emotional guy, sensitive and loving."

She also recognizes how the same openness was manifest in her mother, not least the way she spoke about human behavior. "Hearing her talk about our patterns—how similar we are but with these little differences, and how we communicate can cause so much pain and suffering, but also joy—" she muses, "I'm always very fascinated by humans, and how love can completely change a human being. How something that is completely irrational to you when you're not in love becomes so rational when you are, because love does something to you."

(previous)   Nilsson wears a jacket and skirt by WE11DONE, earrings by SOPHIE BUHAI and rings by J. HANNAH.

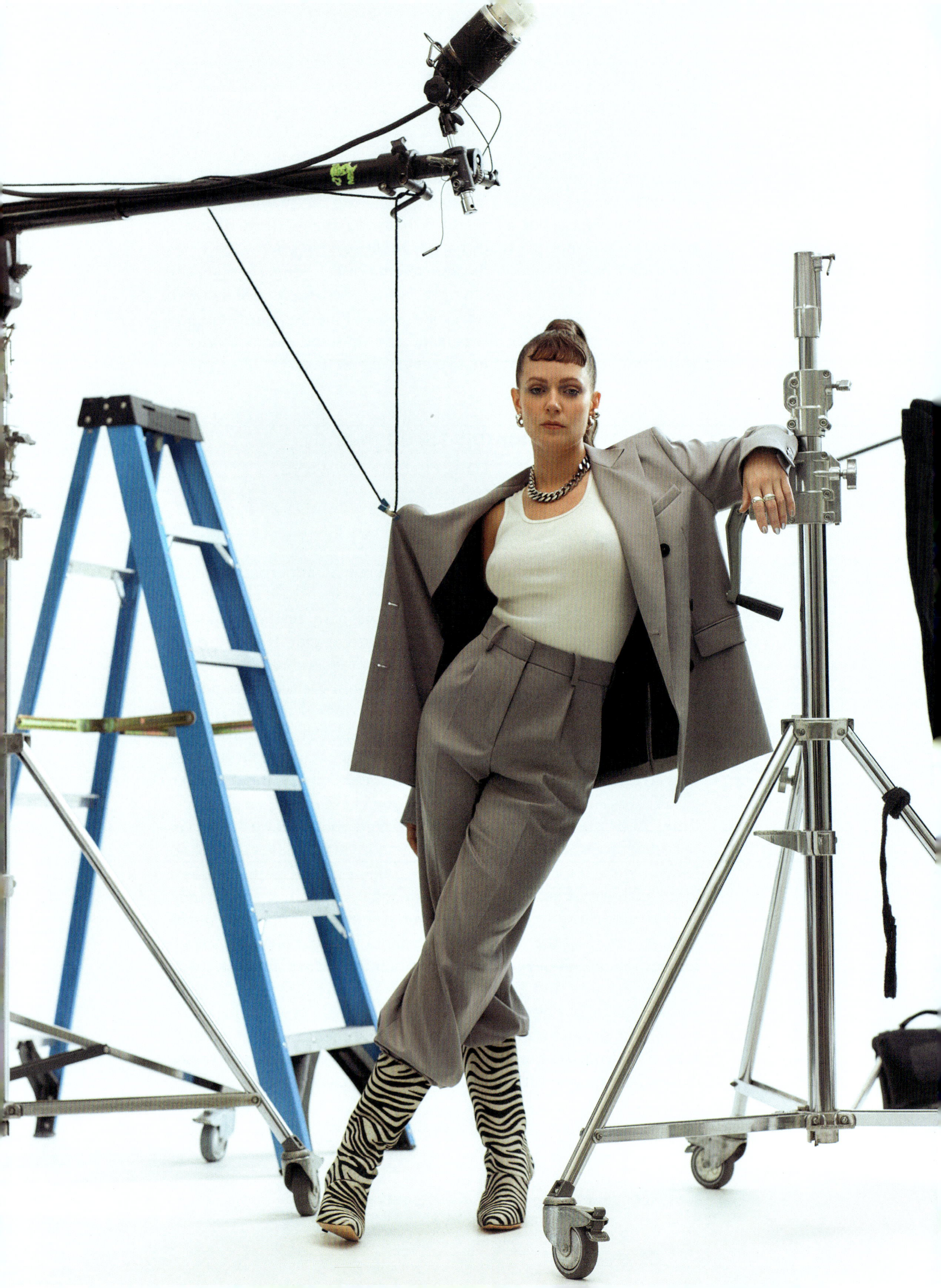

In her most recent releases, Nilsson grapples with the spirals of emotion caused by exposing yourself to the vulnerabilities of love. It's palpable in the catastrophizing that runs through the tracks on *Dirt Femme*, and on the 2023 single "Borderline," where the point of view is from someone inventing all kinds of internal drama with a partner out of insecurity. "With jealousy and insecurity, the only person you're hurting is you," she says. "But for me, it helps to get it out of my head—to say it to a friend, or to my husband, or to put it in a song." She recounts how a friend had interpreted the nightmarish jealousy scenario Nilsson invented for the song "Mistaken" (from her 2019 album *Sunshine Kitty*) to be true. "I played it at a show, and the friend turned to [my husband] and was like, *What did you do to her?!* It's just me feeling vulnerable and insecure in my head and writing a song about it, but it sounds like it's his fault," she giggles. "It's the power of the mind!"

> " Maybe the way I express myself, for some people, is like, *Oh, why would you admit to that feeling?*"

Still, despite being a tool for catharsis, writing is not always something that comes easily. "I've always preferred listening to music that described the feeling, not how I *should* be feeling—aspirational songs telling me what I should aim for," she says. "I just wanted to sit in my feelings and relate to someone, so maybe that's why I write in that way." And yet, despite having been doing it for the best part of two decades, there are still times when Nilsson doubts her ability: "It's going from that place of, *This is shit, I am shit, why does everyone think I can do this?* to *This is great, this is amazing, I can't believe I get to do this!*" As with all things, the way she gets herself through is by reminding herself that "this will pass."

Nilsson does not know what the future holds, but she knows she always wants to be writing songs she relates to. In doing so, and in baring parts of herself so readily, she works to eradicate ingrained feelings of shame, exercising the power of her mind, all while imploring listeners to feel pleasure and tap into their own dark and twisted fantasies, reclaiming desire and autonomy in a way that is fulfilling rather than destructive.

Or, as she puts it, far more succinctly: "You can be deep and still be a slut."

(opposite)   Nilsson wears a suit and boots by IRO, rings by J. HANNAH, ear cuff by FARIS, a vintage top, her own earrings and the stylist's own necklace.

(The Artist)

Karin Mamma

WORDS   EMILY NATHAN
PHOTOGRAPHY   STAFFAN SUNDSTRÖM
STYLING   NAOMI ITKES

ANDERSSON

Inside the moody, mysterious world of Sweden's preeminent painter.

(above)   Andersson at her studio in Stockholm's SoFo neighborhood, with works under production for a new exhibition at David Zwirner Gallery in Paris opening in October 2023.

The Swedish painter Karin "Mamma" Andersson is reluctant to recount how she got her name. "Everybody always asks me about that, so it's boring to me now," she says, and launches into the tale, making me promise that I'll keep it to myself. It's a good story, and it takes us back to her art-school days as a bright-eyed fugitive from the country's dark north—a lonely girl who found her place in the big, cold city. At the heart of the story is a kernel of amiable perversity, a mischievous refusal to do what's proper or what's expected, and it's there that I discover a foundational truth about her, an essential characteristic that can be found blossoming throughout her saturated, soulful canvases: Mamma Andersson is an outlaw.

You'd never know it, by looking at her. In a vintage blouse and leather lace-ups, her hair parted neatly in the middle and twinkling eyes framed by large plastic rims, she appears wholesome rather than contrarian; bookish rather than bold. But she speaks with surprising frankness, betraying her insecurities in an offhand, lighthearted kind of way, and peppers her narratives with anecdotes of subtle resistance.

When I arrive at her Stockholm studio on a sunny day in April, Andersson is not wearing pants, despite a photographer and his assistants huddled behind the lens of a camera on a tripod. "Sorry," she says with a roll of her eyes, pulling on a pair of wrinkled jeans. "I'll be decent now. You wouldn't believe what they brought me for this photo shoot—oversize jackets in crazy colors, what all the Stockholm ladies are wearing.

"If you work with art, you take the water from your own well."

I don't like how they all look the same. But I did recently see the film *Tar*, and I had a big problem after because I felt, *Oh, I'm so masculine! I must do something to be more feminine.*" Having completed the thought out loud, she buries her face in her hands.

Andersson is arguably Sweden's most famous contemporary artist. Since breaking into the American market with a show at David Zwirner Gallery in New York, she has conquered the international landscape, winning the Carnegie Art Award, representing Scandinavia at the Venice Biennale, and joining the permanent collections of such hallowed institutions as New York's MoMA, the Centre Pompidou in Paris, MOCA in LA and Stockholm's Moderna Museet.

For the past 13 years, she has worked in this airy atelier occupying the bottom floor of a lemon-yellow building between a kindergarten and a park in the Swedish capital. Flanked by windows, the space overflows with books, which are stacked and piled on ceiling-high bookshelves or spread open on the paint-splattered floor. There are easels against walls, easels under windows and

KINFOLK

149

(opposite)   Andersson's latest paintings have been inspired by large 18th-century mirrors.

tables dripping with pigment: oil paints in thick, creamy chunks; a rainbow of acrylic tubes, crudely arranged. A collector, Andersson has staged altars around the room, modest vignettes of meaningful objects that provide both atmosphere and inspiration.

What makes her work remarkable is the color, the vision, the downright painterliness of it all; her large, heavy canvases pulse with texture in dreamlike figurations that evoke the great painters of the past. But her similarity with her predecessors stops there. While she might be described as an expressive impressionist, teasing gestures from books or paintings into domestic tableaux and panoramic landscapes that reflect the world around her, Andersson's paintings do not celebrate or idealize. There is no romance in her rich compositions, and though they do seem to integrate some fantastical dream state with familiar motifs from a catalogue of shared cultural references, they always provoke the unsettling feeling that something is awry. Her skies are shaded an eerie, apocalyptic pink that tingles with storm; the light is glaring, without shadow; her lakes are bottomless. Hauntingly beautiful, her paintings are suffused with darkness.

Andersson was born in 1962 in Norrland—the northernmost and least populated of Sweden's territories. In the Western imagination, this remote Nordic region represents desolation, a vast accumulation of sprawling tundras and mysterious folklore where the endless days of summer melt into the eternal darkness of winter. With its dramatic seasons and infinite space, this landscape was the backdrop for what she describes as a "very ordinary" childhood,

> "If you're scared of something, you're also curious."

one lacking in the textbook turmoil that might make somebody "interesting." But just consider what it's produced: Her paintings beg for psychoanalysis.

"If you're scared of something, you're also curious, fascinated by it—and I have been scared of the dark my whole life," Andersson reflects, chronicling a youth complete with all the trappings of health and happiness: supportive, creative parents; a sister; a summerhouse; friends and activities. It's safe to hazard that in the absence of circumstantial struggles, Andersson has created her own ghosts, fleeing the easy, complacent brightness of her upbringing and seeking the anxiety of the unknown. "In a way, I think I have always been listening with an adult's eyes and ears," she says, "even when I was too young. My parents gave me a lot of freedom, but I felt that it was just lonely space. And they never understood why I ran away."

Her preoccupation with the dark side of things is evident in all of her paintings, throbbing beneath their gorgeous surfaces like a heartbeat. Take the canvas *About a Girl*, from 2005, an ostensibly benign snapshot of eight young women—her schoolmates— sitting together around a coffee table. This canvas, Andersson confesses, has brought more than one child to tears. And it is truly nightmarish: Staring blankly out from empty eyes, irises so blue that they bleed into the white, the girls evoke witches, their faces twisted into enigmatic smiles, their hair pierced by thick strokes of black. Behind them, through the window, a putrid green landscape crawls with shadows.[1]

The title promises a picture of a pretty Swede, but the image delivers a visualization of something broken, something lost. "In a group of girls, you can feel the hierarchy between them, and it's a very fragile balance," Andersson explains. "I remember being there at that table with my friends, and the

---

(1)   In *Frieze*, the writer Ronald Jones wrote that *About a Girl* was arguably Andersson's "masterpiece." He mooted that the painting reflects similar themes to a Kurt Cobain song of the same name in which the singer resists the commitment that would save a wobbling relationship.

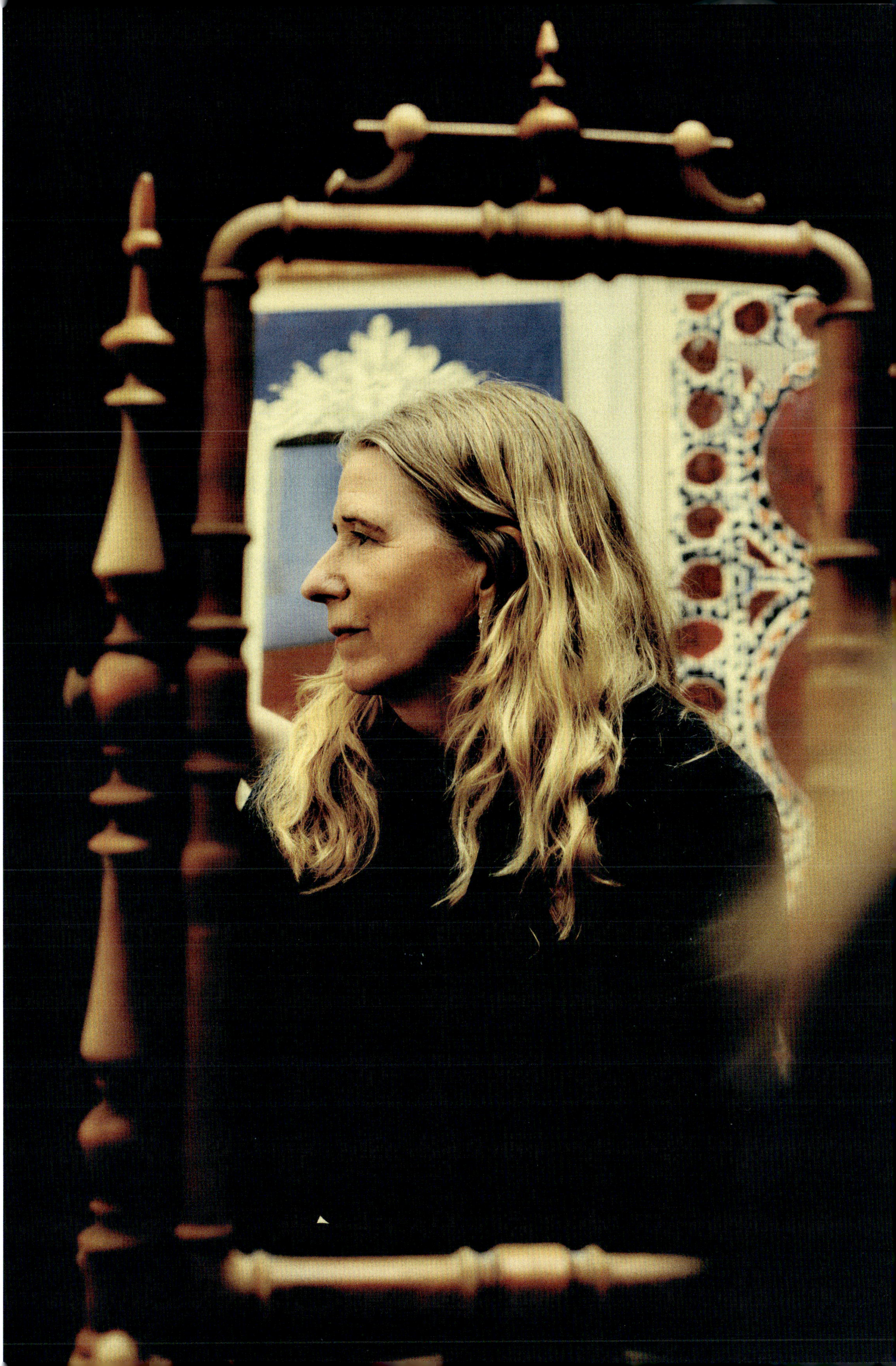

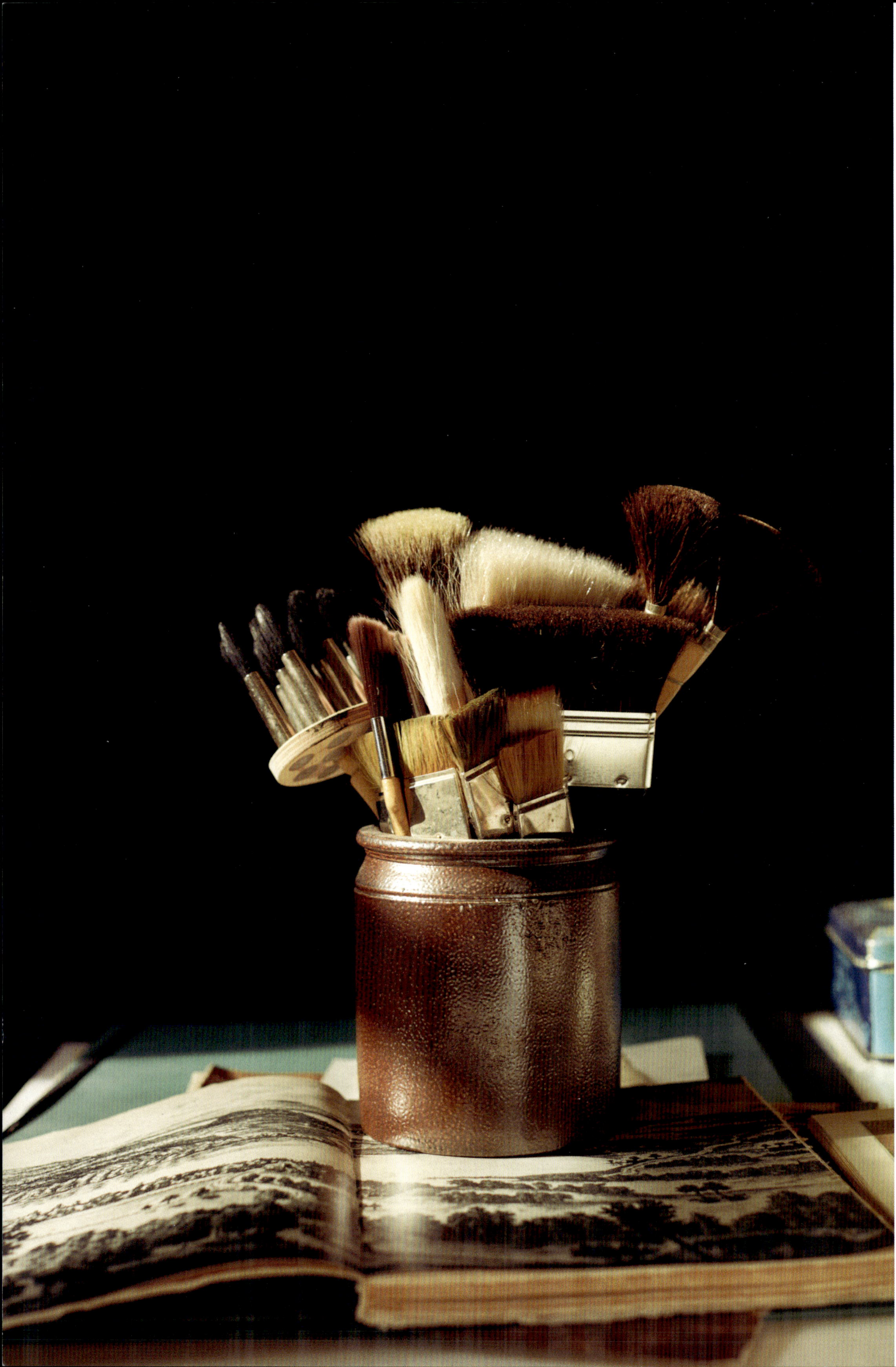

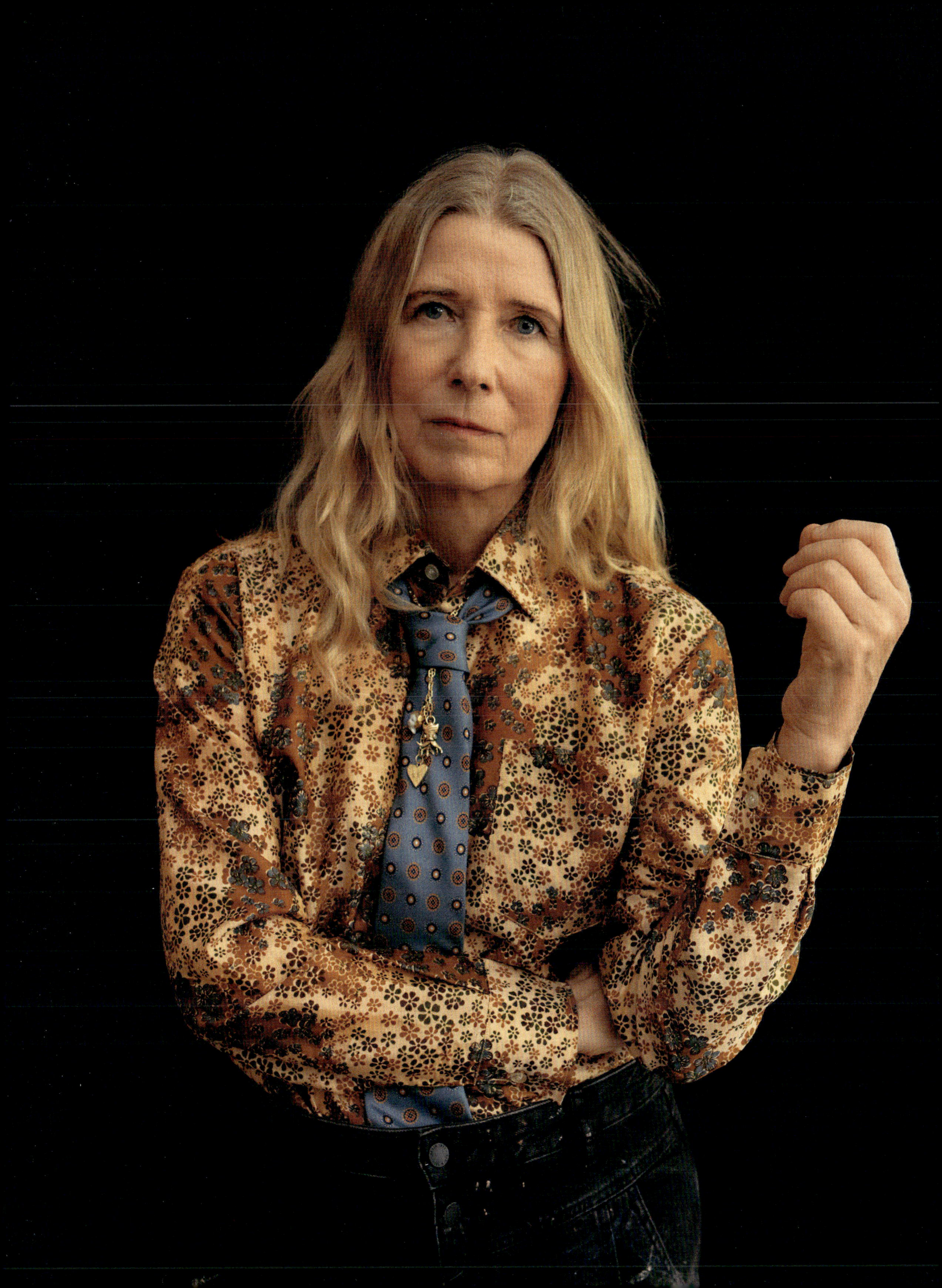

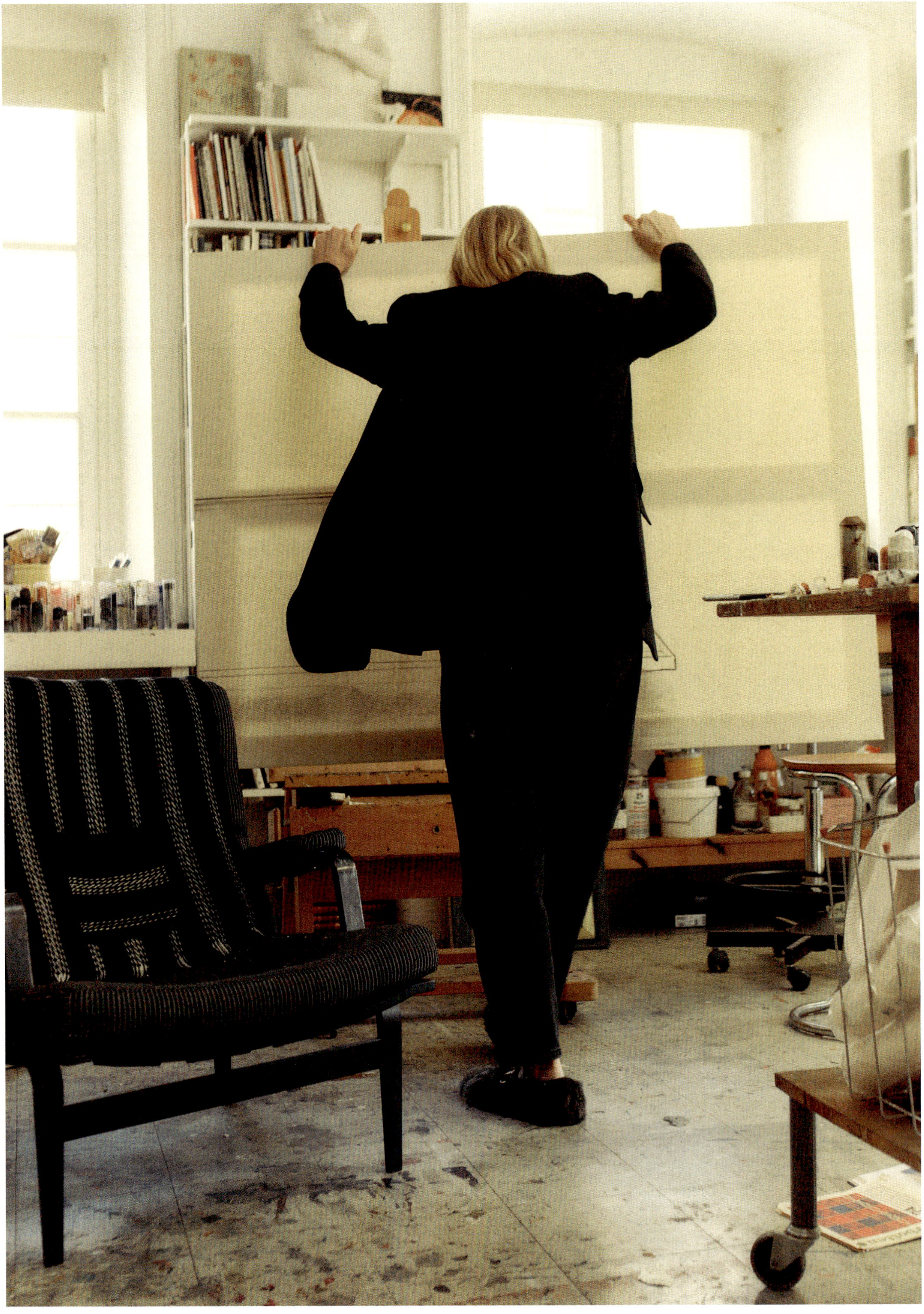

feeling of utter isolation. They're together but they're alone, all of them."

When arriving in Stockholm by plane, the bones and silhouettes of Andersson's paintings reveal themselves like fossils: aerial views of lakes snaking between hillsides, red farmhouses surrounded by mahogany-tipped brush, and stands of trees, their shadows jutting into the water. Trains disappear under craggy rock and emerge again into ochre stretches of ground; pines mingle with the brown spindles of bare trunks. There is forest, too, thick and deep—even the airport is fringed by forest. For a country so civilized, there is something wild about it: The sheer scale of the landscape is overwhelming.

"If you work with art, you take the water from your own well," Andersson tells me, when I ask why she has described every painting as a self-portrait. "And of course, you can borrow water from other people's well, but the main source is coming from yourself. I'm often asked if I have a plan for my paintings, but I don't. I walk in and see the rug I painted yesterday and I think, Okay, I need a floor under the rug. Or, that rabbit must have fur—it's too flat. Or, these colors are not so good together. I see what's there, and I respond to it. It's an intuitive thing, but to be intuitive, you have to trust yourself. And that takes time."

These days, her studio is filled with canvases she's creating for an upcoming show at David Zwirner Gallery in Paris. "Ah, the empty rooms," she sighs. Indeed, the paintings depict moody, grand spaces, interiors and exteriors, reflected in surfaces that echo to infinity—all of them devoid of life. She says that she's recently been fascinated by large, 18th-century mirrors whose size required the junction of two panes, producing a distorting seam in the middle, and that they continue to make an appearance in her art. "These rooms and these warped reflections just seem to be what's coming out right now," she adds, gesturing toward a collage of reference images on the wall: a Japanese block print of a geisha; wallpaper patterns. "And it's a metaphor, probably. I'm just letting the process tell me where to go."

At lunchtime, we make our way across the park to Post Bar, a neighborhood diner where Andersson eats three times a week. She greets the waitresses warmly, and we're seated in a booth. Over steamed fish and potatoes, she orders a beer and speaks wistfully about motherhood, her parents, her sons, until a game of tag between a bird and a rat on a pile of dirt outside the window ensorcells her. "Magpies are very smart, you know; the bird is taunting the rat on purpose!" she says, and stops to watch them as we leave, her eyes gleaming with approval.

Back at the studio, she invites me to join her on the couch for a slice of cardamom cake. "I think my way of working has really changed," she says, unprompted. "I do much more by hand, and don't use so much reference—it makes you secure in one way, but insecure in another. You lean on the picture, but it's better to lean on yourself." A magpie of sorts, Andersson has spent her life establishing a homemade archive of found photographs that she has historically used as inspiration, copying an element from an image and using it as "the entrance into a painting." But in recent years, she tells me, she prefers to rely on her own interior aesthetic world, and has become confident enough to trust her instincts—no matter what shape they might take on the canvas.

"Many of the artists I appreciate most, like Guston or Van Gogh, didn't care if it looked right or not," Andersson says, gazing at a series of black-and-white photographs on the wall. They are portraits of the artists who mean the most to her: Paul Gaugin, the writer Gustaf Fröding, Edvard Munch, Henri Matisse, Picasso, Dick Bengtsson, Yoko Ono, Pippi Longstocking—and the Marx Brothers. "It's something very beautiful and simple when you are not correct. You can have much more experience than painting precisely after a photograph, making porcelain so real you could touch it. That can be very nice, but it can also be very uninteresting, because the reality is always there in front of us. I think what we need, what we *really* need, is the fantasy."

" To be intuitive, you have to trust yourself. And that takes time."

(overleaf)
Andersson wears a suit jacket from TEURN STUDIOS, a tie from STENSTRÖMS and slippers from ALAÏA, plus pieces from her own wardrobe and the stylist's own archive.

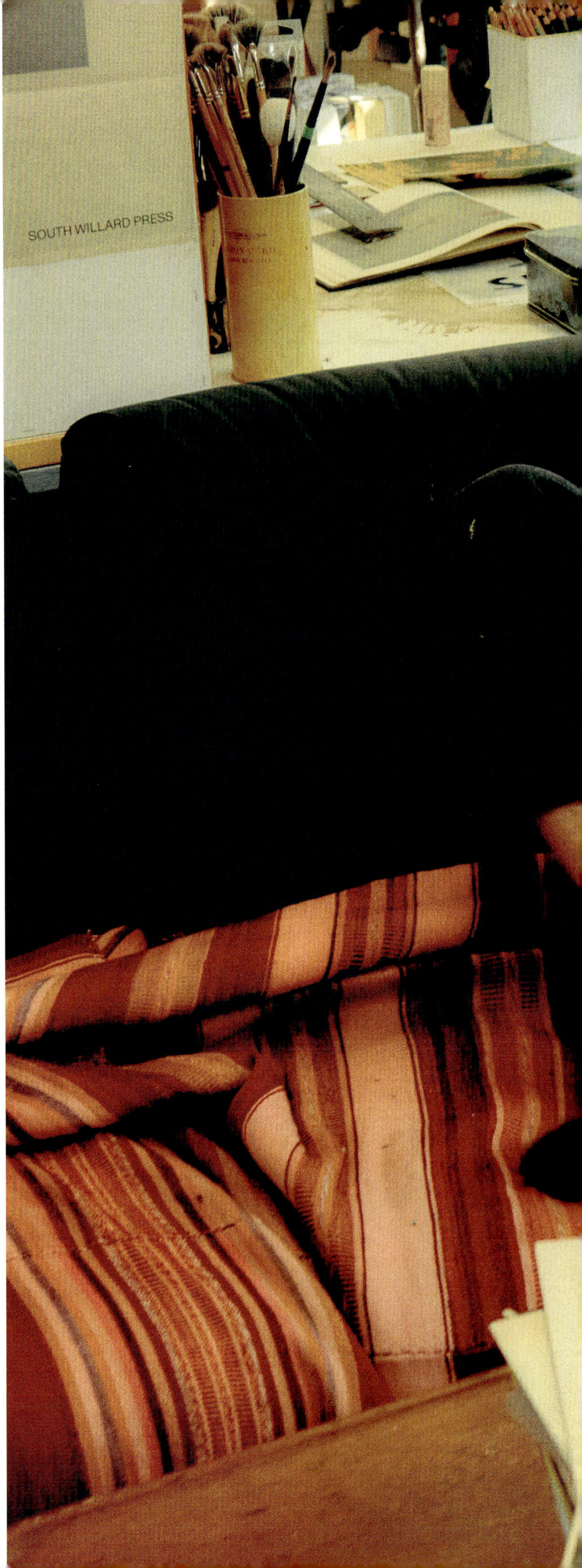
SOUTH WILLARD PRESS

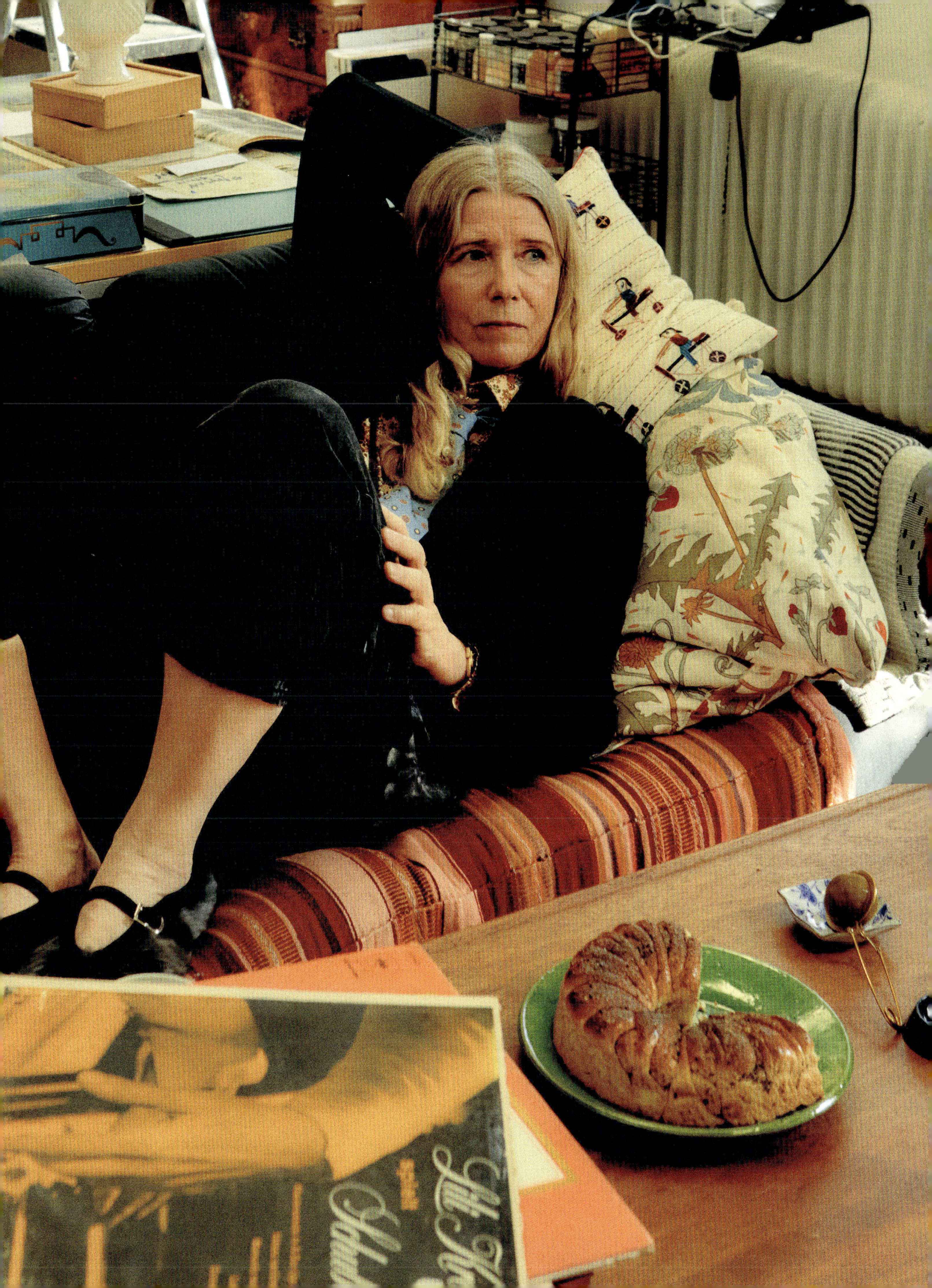

Fares FARES

WORDS	LIV LEWITSCHNIK
PHOTOGRAPHY	ALIXE LAY
STYLING	ANNA SUNDELIN

(The Actor)

After almost 25 years, the master actor steps behind the camera.

Fares Fares leans back on the sofa at his wife Clara Hallencreutz's art studio. We're in Stockholm, where the warmth and light of early summer have hit with full force and the city is heaving with people out enjoying it all.

The Swedish actor has recently wrapped shooting on *A Day and a Half*, his directorial debut due to premiere this fall, and he's clearly proud of the work. "Acting is fascinating, but with directing I get to tell the story my way," he says.

Fares became a name in Sweden after starring as Roro, a park cleaner whose parents want to marry him off, in the 2000 movie *Jalla! Jalla!*—a low-budget production shot by his brother, Josef. They cowrote the movie over the course of a couple of weeks with their friend Torkel Petersson, who also stars in it. It became a sensation on release—the public and critics loved it, with the latter even going so far as to claim it as part of a new wave of Swedish cinema in its portrayal of a side of Sweden few had at that time seen on the big screen.

Since then, Fares has acted in everything from stage shows to music videos to the American television series *Westworld*. Recently, he co-developed and stars in the Swedish hit crime thriller *Partisan*, which delves into the dysfunction and dark secrets of an organic farming cult. Then there are the 27 feature movies that Fares has appeared in, which include big name blockbusters such as Kathryn Bigelow's *Zero Dark Thirty* and Swedish director Daniel

(opposite)   Fares wears a T-shirt by UNNA, a knit and boots by J. LINDEBERG, a jacket by HUGO BOSS, trousers by EYTYS and a scarf by MEHROTRA.
(previous)   He wears a suit by HOPE and a T-shirt by JEANERICA.

Espinosa's *Easy Money* and *Safe House*, all of which have helped catapult Fares onto the global stage. (Although he doesn't exactly see it that way: He describes the experience of trying to make it in Los Angeles as "a slog—never-ending auditions and crap. For a really long time.")

A Day and a Half is a love story turned kidnap chase set in the Swedish countryside. In the movie, Artan (played by Alexej Manvelov, whom Fares acted alongside in the HBO series *Chernobyl*) takes his ex-wife, Louise (Finnish actor Alma Pöysti), hostage in the hopes of reuniting with their daughter. The idea came from a real-life incident that had been percolating in Fares' mind for some time. "There was something that drew me to the tragedy of two people who love each other, but then things go wrong, and a child ends up in between," he explains.

Although Fares didn't initially want to act in the film ("I couldn't be bothered to change into costume"), he ended up playing the police officer who tails the couple on their high-stakes road trip. "You can't tell if a film fully follows your vision before you've cut it and watched it through," he says. "But I'm determined and know what I want—and I won't stop until I have it."

Sitting opposite Fares—tall, angular, bordering on brooding—it's easy to imagine this to be true, until, with a smile, he adds quickly: "Not in a demonic kind of way or anything." Fares seems to have his radar switched on at all times—as if he can feel

"I'm determined and know what I want—and I won't stop until I have it."

(1) Fares stars as a detective in another of Saleh's thrillers, *The Nile Hilton Incident*. Although set again in Egypt, the plot was actually inspired by the murder of Lebanese singer Suzanne Tamim in Dubai in 2008.

your pulse—and it's an energy that is palpable on-screen. Some 20-plus years into his acting career, he's had enough time to practice channeling "characters that go through change"—the type of role he says he's most drawn to.

Five of the films in his back catalog are Danish productions, including *The Keeper of Lost Causes* in which Fares plays a police officer who digs into cold cases, and for which Fares had to learn Danish. "I'm drawn to challenging work," he says, explaining how he believes experience has taught him to "peel off layers, shed the unimportant stuff," and reach deeper, to make his character true to what he feels they should be.

Watch him in 2022's *Boy from Heaven*, and you'll see what he means. Directed by Fares' longtime friend and creative mentor, the Swedish auteur Tarik Saleh, Fares plays Ibrahim, an Egyptian state security official.[1] That meant mastering Egyptian Arabic for the role, which Fares says was difficult to get right despite speaking Levantine Arabic from his childhood in Lebanon.

Saleh shared the screenplay a year before shooting started, and Fares immediately set to work on developing Ibrahim's character—an odd, slightly creepy yet loving agent who grooms an informant at Al-Azhar University, a storied Islamic institution in Cairo. Fares wanted a slouchy look—suit hanging over shoulders, messy hair, potbelly and thick glasses. "The physical appearance of a character draws you in, then the feelings

KINFOLK

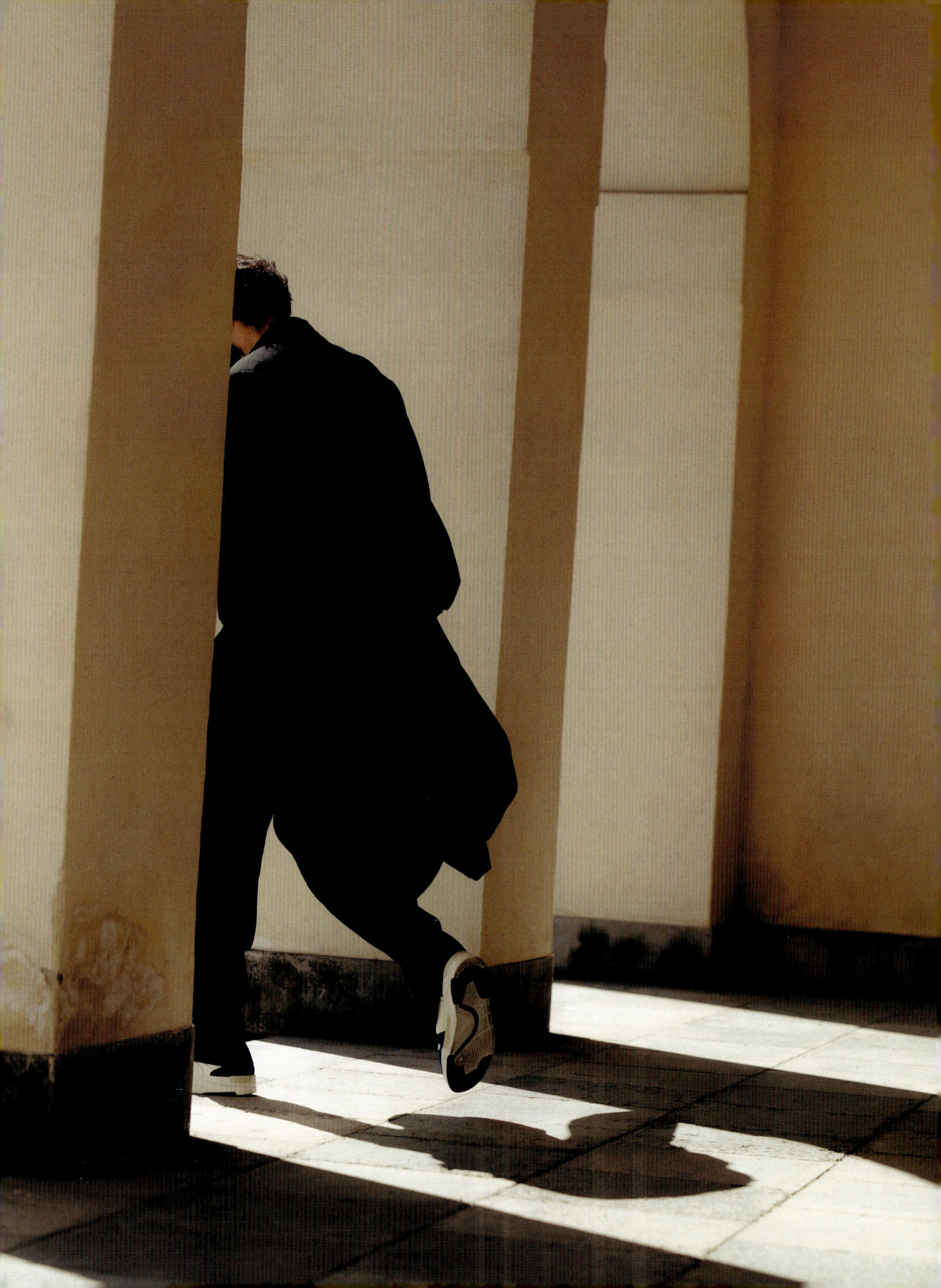

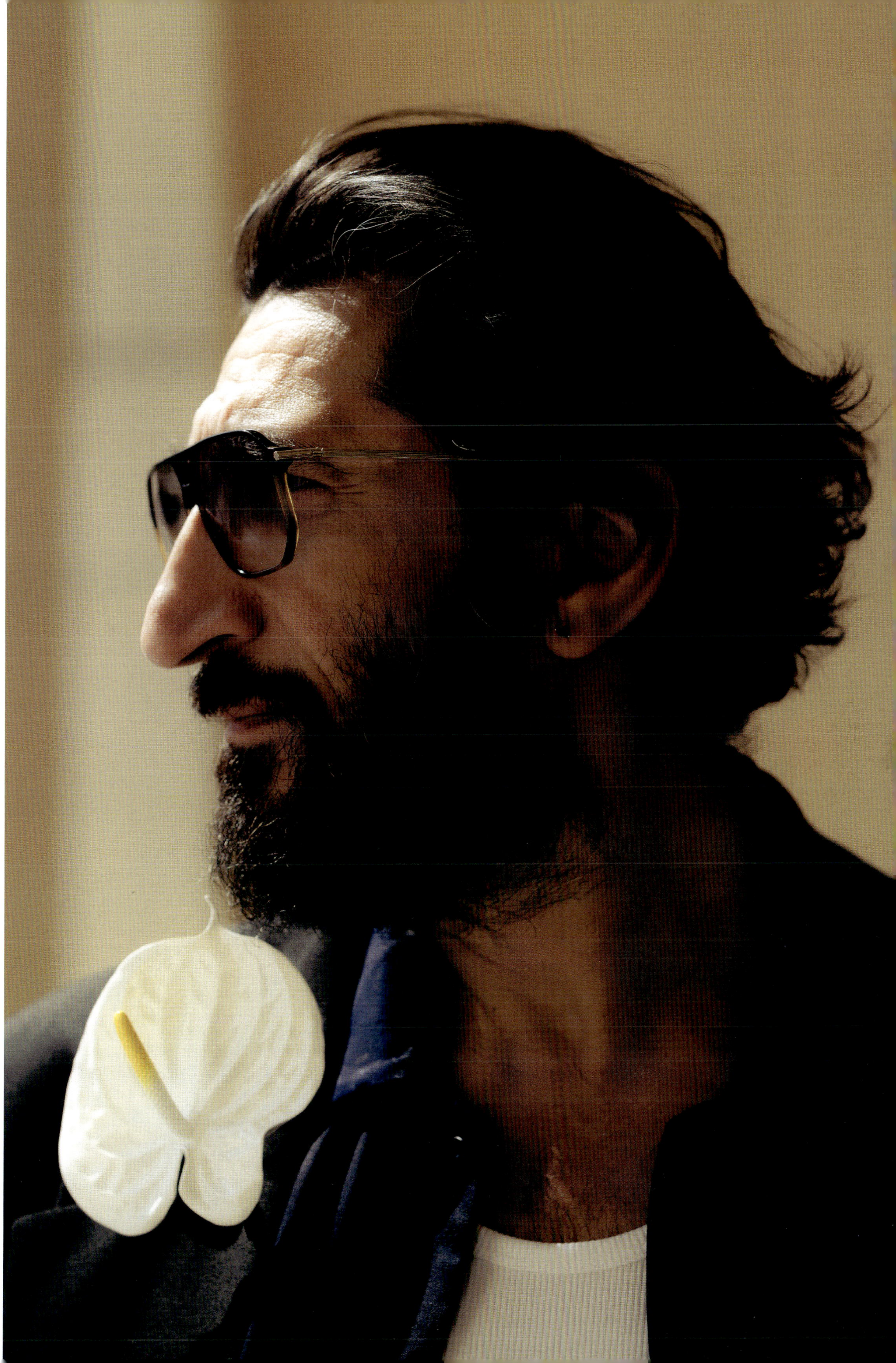

(below)   Fares wears a suit by HOPE, a T-shirt by JEANERICA and boots by EYTYS.
(previous) He wears a coat by HOPE, a shirt, tank top and trousers by CDLP, a brooch by LOEWE and sneakers by GANT.

are switched on," he explains. "I stay with a character for a long time—basically until the next one comes along and kicks the old one out. I do just one at a time, to give it the attention it deserves. They can become so pervasive that I sometimes catch myself walking around at home saying lines from my latest film," he laughs.

> " I stay with a character for a long time—until the next one comes along."

Fares was two when the Lebanese Civil War broke out. Together with his siblings, he spent his childhood between school, home and their parents' hole-in-the-wall business, Peace Bakery. "We sometimes went to the beach, other times we had to run for the bomb shelter," he says. The family fled Lebanon several times and were finally given the right to remain in Sweden (where an aunt had already settled) on the fifth try, when Fares was 14.

He quickly picked up Swedish but the social mores of small-town Örebro in central Sweden baffled him. "I had to figure out which music was right, how to sit right and even spit right in order to fit in," he recalls. In response, Fares shed the image of the good schoolboy, which he had enjoyed and cultivated at home. "That left an empty space," he says. "Theater filled it."

While his parents were happy that Fares was planning to eventually become an architect, he ended up choosing theater school in Gothenburg. "No one thinks you're going to make it in this industry, and mostly people don't," he says. "I've seen so many broken dreams along the way."

He believes his career has benefited from luck and circumstance—and, of course, a certain aptitude for acting. "Not everyone has it," he says. "I think that's true of anything that you dedicate yourself to—it's either a calling or it's not. I'm just glad I found mine."

Between projects, Fares likes to spend time with his wife and their two children at their country house in the Stockholm archipelago, and, he says with a boyish grin creeping across his face, playing Dungeons & Dragons. He is game master over a group of players who meet up every two weeks. "It's crazy fun—," he laughs, "—except for when characters die; that's very stressful."

He spends quite a bit of time prepping maps and characters for each session—this particular "campaign" is two years in the running. After years working at the nexus of acting, directing and writing, Fares is perfectly suited to the game. "It comes down to the same old thing that humans have always been attracted to: sitting around a campfire telling stories, and living inside the heads of fictional characters," he says. "It's a complex world that requires attention to every little detail."

RU BEN

Crude, contrary—and killing it: Meet the auteur of awkwardness.

(The Director)

WORDS — ELLE HUNT
PHOTOGRAPHY — SINA ÖSTLUND

ÖSTLUND

THE FEEL-BAD FILMMAKER IS BREAKING THROUGH.

There are very few scenarios that Ruben Östlund can't turn into a social experiment. When the Swedish filmmaker first started flying business class, for example, he noticed himself eating more slowly, holding himself with greater control and behaving in general "a little bit more sophisticated," he admits.

Östlund quotes from psychological papers like they are knock-knock jokes, and passes on insights into human behavior as if engrossed in irresistible gossip about mutual friends. One of his favorite findings is that people would prefer to give themselves an electric shock than be left alone with their thoughts.

"I think sociology is hilarious," he says. Östlund's work, as a writer and director, is like a rollicking game of "Would you rather?" with the most clued-in, whip-smart crowd you know. His movies test audiences' sympathies, challenge their assumptions and dare them to confront the contradictions in their thinking.

In *Force Majeure*, for example—Östlund's breakout feature from 2014—a couple grapples with the aftermath of a father and husband's split-second decision, in the face of an apparent avalanche, to abandon his family. In *The Square*, masculinity and privilege are warped by the surreal lens of contemporary art. *Triangle of Sadness*, his English-language debut, contrasts the world of the rich and beautiful with a gleefully gross second act when a luxury cruise ship encounters rough seas.[1]

For all three movies, Östlund was the sole writer and director—and his star has ascended steadily with each. Having won the Palme d'Or himself with *Triangle of Sadness* in 2022, Östlund returned to Cannes this year as a judge. He approached the panel prepared to push boundaries: "The most boring thing is consensus," he declared at the opening of the festival—though, as president of the jury, Östlund was tasked with reaching just that.

When we speak at the end of May, one week after the festival's close, he acknowledges the apparent tension with a rueful laugh. "The presidency is more of being a diplomat, of course, in order to make sure that everybody can say what they want to say.... I'm much more of an agitator, you know?" (That said, he is satisfied with the panel's decision to honor *Anatomy of a Fall*, by the French director Justine Triet.)

Östlund is speaking over Zoom from a kitchen table in Hamburg, where his wife, the fashion photographer Sina Östlund, has a shoot. (They live between Gothenburg and Majorca.) He's just emerged from a lunchtime nap with their young son, Elias, now in the care of a friend off-camera. It's a welcome return to domestic life after the glitz, glamour and rigorous debate of the festival—though that, too, Östlund seemed to approach as fieldwork.

(1) The movie is noted for a 15-minute-long scene in which many of the characters become violently seasick and projectile vomit at the same time as the boat's sewage system erupts.

As president of the jury, he was extended the full red-carpet treatment—including personal security, he says, bemused. "It's been a very interesting experience to go from being in Cannes, and having a driver and a bodyguard for 14 days—to now going with a baby trolley to the playground and taking care of my son."

Östlund's interest in human nature was fostered from an early age by his parents, both teachers. One of his earliest memories, from when he was about 10, is of coming upon a Rolls-Royce while out with his father in Denmark. The driver told them that the angel ornament on the hood had been deliberately removed—too many people had been spitting on it. How times change, observes Östlund: "In the '80s, it was shameful to show off with wealth." (At least in Scandinavia, he adds.)

> " I always try to look for a dilemma: when you have two or more options, but none of them are easy."

Often, these recollections have fed directly into his films. When Östlund was 16, his mother told him about the Asch conformity test, a famous psychological experiment from 1935, which investigated the impact of group pressure. Tasking a group of strangers with solving a straightforward logic problem, it found that one-third of participants would give the answer that was favored by the majority, even if it was clearly incorrect. Östlund's mother was staging the experiment with her students. "I was thinking: 'How can you do this?" he says. "But I couldn't forget about it."

Decades later, the theme of peer pressure informs the premise of Östlund's 2007 film *Involuntary*.[2] At a scene level, too—instead of relying on conflict to drive the narrative, or the now-ubiquitous "trauma plot," centering on characters' historic hardships—Östlund taps that powder keg of social mores. "I always try to look for a dilemma: when you have two or more options, but none of them are easy," he says. "It's not about who the individuals are; it's about a human being dealing with a specific situation or setup."

For Östlund, films can highlight our common humanity, even where it's not expected—and especially where it's somewhat ridiculous. What bores him most are stories about psychopaths, "because the problem is already solved from the beginning: We have to catch that person and put them behind bars," he says with a shrug. "I love when the stakes are socially dangerous, rather than physically dangerous."

[2] Group dynamics makes its way into the five interweaving narratives at the heart of *Involuntary*, as when a schoolteacher gives her students a lesson about not going along with the majority, but subsequently finds herself under peer pressure in the staff room.

He argues that audiences, too, find it easier to invest in a precise, interpersonal premise such as the marital fault lines abruptly—and excruciatingly—exposed in *Force Majeure*. That film drew from Östlund's years of experience in early adulthood, working at ski resorts in the Alps. It was there that he started making ski films, which later gained him admission to film school. "I didn't come from a cinema background—that was how I got my 10,000 hours of practice," he says.

When Östlund graduated in 2001, he was steeped in the French New Wave movement—prized by his teachers—and inspired by the Dogme 95 realist filmmaking more recently pioneered in Denmark by director Lars von Trier.[3] Filmmaking, to Östlund, was a technical or aesthetic challenge; it wasn't until a decade later that he began to understand the importance of bringing his audience with him.

For the premiere of his film *Play*, at the 2011 Cannes Film Festival, Östlund was seated behind a couple who made no attempt to conceal their impatience with his six-minute-long opening scene. Östlund imitates the man's heavy sigh, dramatic eye roll, his head lolling in his chair. "It was a very painful moment," he says. But it also made him realize that he wanted his films to engage people as much as they challenged them.

"I started to think that I had made a typical, genre, European art house film and I wanted to break free from that—I wanted to make films that were wild and entertaining, and thought-provoking at the same time . . . films that I'd actually want to watch myself," he says.

In setting out to please himself, Östlund has garnered his greatest critical and commercial successes yet. *The Square* and *Triangle of Sadness* won the Palme d'Or at Cannes in 2017 and 2022, making Östlund only the ninth director to have ever been honored twice. But in the past year alone, Östlund's work has reached his biggest, broadest audience yet, with *Triangle of Sadness* grossing $38.2

(3) Dogme 95 was a Danish avant-garde movement created by Lars von Trier with the intent of "purifying" filmmaking by refusing to use special effects and post-production. The ten commandments in its manifesto were referred to as the "Vow of Chastity."

He argues that audiences, too, find it easier to invest in a precise, interpersonal premise such as the marital fault lines abruptly—and excruciatingly—exposed in *Force Majeure*. That film drew from Östlund's years of experience in early adulthood, working at ski resorts in the Alps. It was there that he started making ski films, which later gained him admission to film school. "I didn't come from a cinema background—that was how I got my 10,000 hours of practice," he says.

When Östlund graduated in 2001, he was steeped in the French New Wave movement—prized by his teachers—and inspired by the Dogme 95 realist filmmaking more recently pioneered in Denmark by director Lars von Trier.[3] Filmmaking, to Östlund, was a technical or aesthetic challenge; it wasn't until a decade later that he began to understand the importance of bringing his audience with him.

For the premiere of his film *Play*, at the 2011 Cannes Film Festival, Östlund was seated behind a couple who made no attempt to conceal their impatience with his seven-minute-long opening scene. Östlund imitates the man's heavy sigh, dramatic eye roll, his head lolling in his chair. "It was a very painful moment," he says. But it also made him realize that he wanted his films to engage people as much as they challenged them.

"I started to think that I had made a typical, genre, European art house film and I wanted to break free from that—I wanted to make films that were wild and entertaining, and thought-provoking at the same time . . . films that I'd actually want to watch myself," he says.

In setting out to please himself, Östlund has garnered his greatest critical and commercial successes yet. *The Square* and *Triangle of Sadness* won the Palme d'Or at Cannes in 2017 and 2022, making Östlund only the ninth director to have ever been honored twice. But in the past year alone, Östlund's work has reached his biggest, broadest audience yet, with *Triangle of Sadness* grossing $26 million

(3) Dogme 95 was a Danish avant-garde movement created by Lars von Trier with the intent of "purifying" filmmaking by refusing to use special effects and post-production. The ten commandments in its manifesto were referred to as the "Vow of Chastity."

at the global box office off the back of its three Oscar nominations.[4] Its provocative campaign (with the headline "Wealthy people of privilege: this film is about you"), emphasized Östlund's reputation as the court jester or Shakespearean fool, holding a mirror up to power to reveal a far-from-flattering reflection.

But it highlights a growing tension: As his profile rises and his films venture further mainstream, Östlund moves closer to the institutions that he seeks to skewer. *Triangle of Sadness* received an eight-minute standing ovation at Cannes, despite—or perhaps because of—its merciless satirizing of the ultra-rich.

For an armchair sociologist like Östlund, each screening has been fascinating. One audience member, at a viewing in Paris, was vocal with his complaint that the film's portrayal of the rich was "too simple." Östlund chuckles: "It turns out he was one of the richest guys in France, like a billionaire—so I'm happy that he got upset."

> "I don't consider myself more or less privileged than the main characters."

At other times, the response has been perplexing—such as when Östlund was invited to speak at a screening of *Triangle of Sadness*, held as a charitable fundraiser by a luxury cruise company. "That was kind of surprising," he says, laughing. "I have to ask myself if I maybe failed with what I was trying to do."

Östlund is no fan of the one-note "eat the rich" sentiment increasingly being served up by Hollywood, though he has been credited with starting the trend. Often, he says, discussions of inequality place too much emphasis on the individual (though it's true, he adds, that "billionaires don't like to pay taxes"). His intention with *Triangle of Sadness* was to explore class and privilege through the economic and social structures underpinning them.

His understanding of Marxist politics, fostered by his mother, informed Woody Harrelson's role as a communist captain, as well as the highly stratified society of the cruise liner itself, upended when disaster strikes. "The left wing describes society almost in the same way as Hollywood does: The rich capitalist is evil, the poor people in the bottom are genuine and nice," says Östlund.

"It's almost like the left-wingers have forgotten about Marx, you know? Our behavior comes from which position we have in the financial and social structure." That, of course, equally implicates him. "I don't consider myself more or less privileged than the main characters," he says.

(4) *Triangle of Sadness* was nominated for Best Picture, Best Original Screenplay and Best Director at this year's Academy Awards.

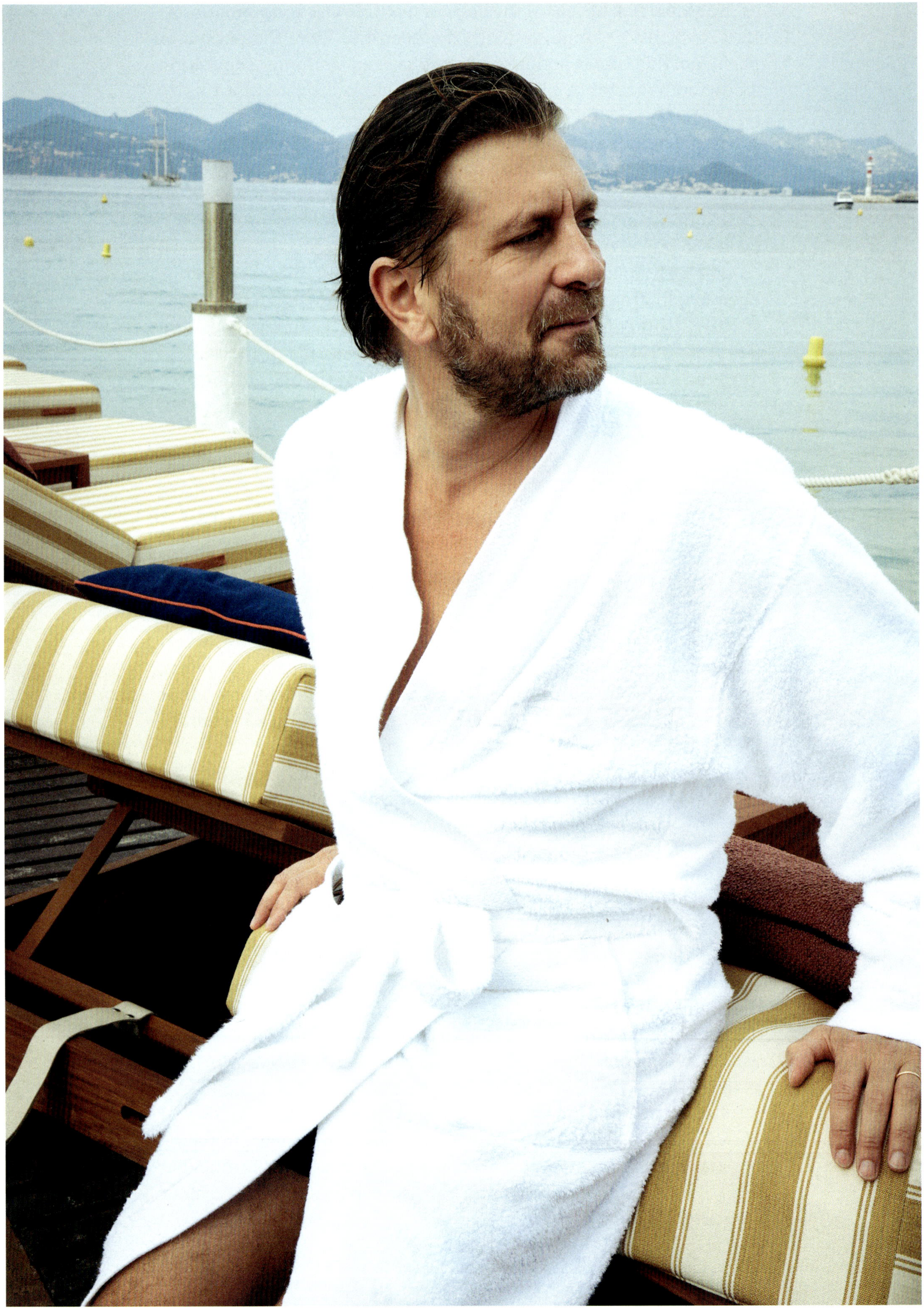

That, to Östlund, is the great power of cinema as sociological lens: It can show people as we are, shedding light on the hidden influences on our behaviors and beliefs, and allow us to process it together. With *Triangle of Sadness*, Östlund sought to create a collective experience, in defiance of the siloed, solo streaming so common today. "I wanted the audience to feel like they were on a roller coaster ride, watching it together when they went to the cinema."

However, some critics, particularly in the US, reviewed *Triangle of Sadness* as a blunt anti-rich diatribe.[5] It is "of course" frustrating when his nuance is flattened or intent misread—but not unexpected, he says, in a climate that can be inclined to shy from both personal responsibility and creative risk. "Because I was leaving the Swedish language and going over to English, I felt that I had to punch much harder in order to push the humor," says Östlund. (*Downhill*, the 2020 American remake of *Force Majeure*, starring Will Ferrell and Julia Louis-Dreyfus, smooths Östlund's sharp comedy down to a nub.)

His own measure of failure is relative, he says: "If I can't identify with the character's behavior, then I've failed. I have to see the possibility of their actions myself. Otherwise, I don't want to go there." With research, Östlund says he was able to empathize with even the most reprehensible rich passengers on *Triangle of Sadness* (though he admits: "It was kind of hard sometimes").

Östlund's personal outlook on humanity is more positive than his films may suggest, he says. "We're really good at collaborating and taking care of each other; we are really focused on trying to create an equal society. My films just focus on when we're failing," he adds with a smile.

Far from being absorbed into the establishment, success seems to be only making Östlund more daring. After the indirect social experiment of screening *Triangle of Sadness* at Cannes, for his next film, Östlund intends to stage an actual provocation.

(5) *The New York Times* reviewer A.O. Scott wrote a particularly scathing critique, calling the movie "a preening, obvious satire of contemporary hypocrisy" and "a shaggy-dog art-house reboot of *Gilligan's Island*."

He is currently in the early stages of writing the script for *The Entertainment System Is Down*. The setup is classic Östlund: With Harrelson once again as their captain, a group of passengers settle into a long-haul flight only to discover that they have no on-board entertainment, internet or digital distractions. Östlund describes it as a "disaster movie": "I'm so happy with the premise," he says, delightedly.

As the characters ration a tablet's remaining charge, or seek to distract combustible young children, those in the theater will similarly have their patience tested. True to the electric shock experiment on "the disengaged mind," Östlund's hypothesis is that, challenged to sit with their thoughts, his audience will unravel along with the characters. His aim, he says, "is to create the biggest walk-out in the history of the Cannes Film Festival."

> "If I can't identify with the character's behavior, then I've failed."

(above) Östlund was photographed by his wife, Sina Östlund, at Hôtel Martinez in Cannes, France.

Part 4.
DIRECTORY
Clutter, a crossword & an avant-garde art carnival.
178 — 192

178 Object Matters
179 Last Night
180 Róisín Murphy
182 Crossword
183 Correction
186 Cult Rooms
188 Behind the Scenes

OBJECT MATTERS

Words:
Okechukwu Nzelu

A spotlight on commonplace books.

Commonplace books are a little like personalized encyclopedias: places to write down tidbits of knowledge gleaned from the world, like aphorisms, lines of verse, lyrics or memorable movie quotes; they might also include recipes, prayers, portraits, mathematical formulas, maps or anything else useful and easily forgotten. Unlike journals or diaries, these notes are not usually the owner's original thoughts, and thus offer a different kind of window into their mind. In these pages are things perhaps even more intimate than secrets: desires, passions, aspirations.

Arguably, the commonplace book dates back almost 2,000 years. In the second century, Marcus Aurelius' *Meditations* began as his collection of ideas and quotations. Much later, in 14th-century Italy, *zibaldone*, or "hodgepodges," were commonplace books kept by writers and thinkers as a way of recording interesting words and thoughts. The Italian writer Giovanni Boccaccio, a major influence on medieval English poet Geoffrey Chaucer, left behind three, whose contents range from astrology to risqué poems written in Latin.

In England, the books flourished in the 17th century, when university students were increasingly taught and assigned the keeping of them. Many prominent writers kept commonplace books throughout their lives. John Milton's was paginated, indexed and divided into sections on ethics, economics and politics. Philosopher John Locke's guidebook, *A New Method of Making Commonplace-books*, was published at the start of the 18th century and helped spread the practice beyond the academic community. Many people began to record interesting quotations not simply for academic success, but to develop themselves in the burgeoning art of conversation.

Since the Renaissance, writers and thinkers—both amateur and professional—have kept commonplace books too: Enthusiasts include Thomas Hardy, Virginia Woolf and Arthur Conan Doyle (and his fictional creation Sherlock Holmes). Today, Bill Gates' GatesNotes.com acts as a sort of digital commonplace book, collecting his own thoughts alongside those of other writers.

Comparisons are often made between commonplace books and social media platforms like Pinterest, but dedicated apps are also available, such as Bear, Notion and Evernote, alongside more generic note-taking apps like Google Keep and iOS's Notes. In today's information-saturated society, where we have access to so much data and have so few ways of filtering what matters most, it's easy to see the appeal of this kind of record-keeping. But for those who prefer an analog approach, any paper notebook or indexed box of notecards still offers a new opportunity to take up a 2,000-year-old tradition.

LAST NIGHT

Words:
Gabriele Dellisanti

What did gallerist SELMA MODÉER WIKING do with her evening?

Selma Modéer Wiking likes to keep busy. An actor, creative director, curator and graphic designer, she also recently opened the Cowgirl Gallery in the hip Möllan neighborhood of Malmö, Sweden. It's a space she envisions as a hub for local creatives—hosting art exhibitions, music performances and film screenings, while offering guests fresh coffee and snacks. After closing last night, Wiking allowed herself a few hours off.

GABRIELE DELLISANTI: What did you get up to last night?

SELMA MODÉER WIKING: I always say my workday starts when the gallery closes. I spend my days welcoming people in and making sure the place is tidy. Then the real work begins: invoicing, paying bills, scouting artists, preparing for the next day, and so on. But yesterday I managed to squeeze in a night at the cinema!

GD: What did you see?

SMW: A 1988 movie by American director Godfrey Reggio called *Powaqqatsi*. I saw it at Hypnos, a small independent cinema here. I love it. They show films you've never heard of and I like to go once or twice a week. I had also planned to go to a friend's restaurant after the film, but it ended up going on too long, so I didn't make it.

GD: Which restaurant is that?

SMW: It's a place called Rau, not too far from the gallery and my apartment. It serves Korean-inspired dishes. It's so good. Right next to it is my favorite bar in town, Riket, where they have a fantastic selection of natural wines and the staff is always lovely.

GD: How do you like to spend your evenings when you stay in?

SMW: Scouting for new artists to exhibit at the gallery is my favorite pastime. When I go home in the evening, I browse through all the books I have and just get in touch with people I find inspiring. Every time I travel, I make sure to have enough room in my luggage to bring back tons of books and magazines. They're essential for what I do.

Photo: Viggo Hasselquist

DIRECTORY

RÓISÍN MURPHY

Words: Charles Shafaieh

Five questions for an art-pop icon.

For Róisín Murphy, unpredictability is a necessity. Amid the stultifying homogeneity of most contemporary pop and disco, the Irish-born artist's catalog is a rich amalgam of musical styles and cultures, inspired as much by Iggy Pop and Grace Jones as by Laurie Anderson and J.G. Ballard.[1] Her genre-melding predilections echo the diversity of revelers at Manchester and Sheffield clubs in the late 1980s and early '90s, where she immersed herself at just 15 years old by staying put in Manchester, alone, after her parents split up and relocated. Perpetually strong-willed and independent, she reached fame as half of the superstar duo Moloko and has continued delighting her dedicated fan base in her solo career since. Preceding the release of her sixth studio album, *Hit Parade*, she speaks about the necessity of dancing and bravery as well as the unlikely roots of her passion for clubbing.

CHARLES SHAFAIEH: *Hit Parade* opens with "What Not to Do," which challenges us to be brave and dream those dreams we might reject. Why is that call so necessary today?

RÓISÍN MURPHY: Always be brave. It's an essential part of being. That's something I've lived by since I was 15 and made the decision to go it alone. That decisive 15-year-old is still inside me. It takes bravery to be decisive.

There's an awful malaise in the modern world: Being able to communicate instantly through technology has made people less driven by their hearts, less committed. Just to get someone to meet you for coffee can be complicated! We didn't have a telephone in the house when I was a kid. People just walked in the door, sat down, and you had to make them a cup of tea. Everything was much more gut-driven. I still live by that.

Bravery has come up when people see my performances and artwork, when they see me switch musically from one direction to another, when they see I play characters, and that I prioritize that over trying to predict what people might like or want. I don't see it as bravery though, because I don't have the bravery to be fake.

CS: Dancing is gut-driven, a form of letting go that rejects trying to control everything. You've called it a fundamental right. Why is it so important?

RM: I dance every day. I can't help but move to music. I don't play an instrument, and dancing is my gateway to understanding musical arrangement. It's drawing, in a certain sense; it's a 3D graph of the music you're absorbing. When it's predictable—when I can figure out the arrangement before it comes to me—I can't stand it! But if I don't know and have to adjust my dancing, that's when I'm really having fun.

CS: Was Manchester's club culture your first exposure to that kind of event?

RM: In a sense, no. I was brought up around live musicians and would have been at my uncle's jazz bands as a baby. They'd have these all-day events with eight-hour sets on Sundays. These amazing parties had the same essential feeling as the club—of getting together around music, getting drunk, dancing, living, aspiring to something more. Joy was what held it together. My aunts always said to me, "We knew you had the music in you when we saw you dancing to your Uncle Jim's band."

If we were in somebody's living room having a party, everybody would sing, one by one or all together. Everybody knew 100 songs. It was like living in an MGM musical. It was song as a storytelling form that was so essential to that culture in a really natural way—not in a way of wanting to be a superstar but just as part of life, to communicate through previously existing songs. On this record, there's a strain of mortality underneath the joy, a black line underneath the color. I think it comes from seeing that culture go. It's unbelievable. And you don't just mourn the people who are gone but the whole time that has gone.

CS: Another world has died: Teenagers today couldn't live as you did in Manchester, receiving housing benefits to have your own apartment.

RM: It wasn't a perfect apartment—it had an outside toilet—but it was lovely. It was the best decision I ever made. In the UK now, you have to be over 18 to get housing benefits. I would have ended up in foster care or in a shared house with social workers coming and going. But I'm living proof that was the best thing that could ever have happened to me, and I gave back tons to society after that—plenty of tax! [Laughs]

It's confounding to me, when I look back, at how strong I was. But I didn't have anything else except strength. It was worth it, I think, so it's hard for me to get my head around the nanny state and bureaucracy. It's not more efficient.

CS: You never choose the "easy" path.

RM: Everything I do is sincere. I don't create things because I'm thinking about what people want. It's not that I don't want to be successful, and I have an ego, obviously. But I would be ashamed to make anything which I didn't put everything into that I possibly could. I'd be ashamed to make anything that was shit.

(1) J.G. Ballard's story "The Thousand Dreams of Stellavista," about mobile, mood-sensitive houses, inspired Murphy to think about AI and write a song for her latest album, *Hit Parade*.

NOTABLE ACHIEVEMENT

Crossword: Mark Halpin

(NOTE)
In eight squares, the letters from the Across entries and Down entries won't match. Take note of each of these by entering both letters in the square, and then circling it. Also, underline the first letter of the clue for each Across or Down answer containing such a square. When you're finished, the underlined letters, read in clue order, will describe what you've successfully done!

ACROSS

1. Task-switching keyboard combo on PC
7. Sprayed water through a rubber tube
12. Aquatic feat from an Acapulco cliff or Olympic tower
15. Post ___ (after death)
16. Farewell, en français
17. Combatant from Nicaragua, or opposed to
18. Viewing a classical composer in a store's display, with no intent to buy?
20. Six-pack components
23. Fib
24. Ailing, sick
25. Architect I.M.
26. Shark on some menus
28. Ears you might nibble on?
30. Counterpart of "thx," when texting
31. The id, ego, and superego combined
33. Like a rose by another name, smell-wise, per Shakespeare
36. Game where kids search for a classical composer?
38. En masse, liberal or progressive types
40. Like some bombs or super-precise clocks
44. Eternally, to a poet
45. Basis for a lawsuit
47. Continental currency
48. Taylor of fashion
49. Dyspeptic bartender Szyslak of "The Simpsons"
51. Words of hesitation
53. Morning moisture
54. "Classical composer, keep going in the same direction"?
58. Thoroughly implant or establish, as a plant or idea
59. Benevolent, charitable activity
63. Anxiety, jitters
64. "Nor I," informally
65. Household or laundromat appliance
66. Sea foams

DOWN

1. "Eureka!"
2. Simu ___, the first Asian actor to star in a Marvel movie
3. Golfer Woods's entrepreneurial and philanthropic company, aptly
4. Muscle; sinew
5. Motrin alternative
6. Hi-tech optical prosthesis, like the Six Million Dollar Man's
7. Elaborate trouble or commotion
8. Game show choice: "Deal ____ deal?"
9. Have paint applied with light dabs and dots
10. Most creepy
11. Emirati's neighbor in Muscat
13. YouTube offering
14. Suffix with ranch
15. 1250, to Caesar
19. Inveterate boozers
20. Piece of rock concert equipment
21. ___ relief
22. Heavens above
27. Earthy yellow shade
29. Sought help from in an emergency
30. Orange tea type
32. Evil computer of sci-fi filmdom
34. Neighbors in one's airplane row, say
35. Damp
37. Gadget in a library, or one doing Carbon-14 testing
38. Woodworker completing mortise joints
39. Home for poultry
41. Dirty puddle contents
42. Wrath
43. Animal sacred to Hindus
46. Moscow money
48. Thymus or pituitary: prefix
49. Shakespeare's "I, not remembering how I cried out then, will cry ___ again."
50. Ways to escape a dilemma
52. Substitute for real money
55. Slithy one, to Lewis Carroll
56. Viet ___
57. Tutsi's Rwandan foe
60. That guy, in Germany
61. Observe
62. Virginia Woolf's "___ Dalloway"

CORRECTION: CLUTTER

Words:
Ed Cumming

A tidy room does not always beget a tidy mind.

There is a famous Annie Leibovitz photograph of Karl Lagerfeld, taken in 2018, a year before he died. In a high-collared white shirt, his hair almost the same color, the designer appears as a small figure dwarfed by an ocean of papers, books, magazines, files, illustrations and invitations that rise almost to head height, the detritus of a career that never stopped. In the middle of this chaos is Choupette, his cat, looking out at us, somewhat bemused.

Clutter is usually thought of as an obstacle to the creative life. Without order in the physical space, goes the thinking, it is difficult to have the kind of mental calm needed to come up with something new.

Across different fields, the typical advice is to reduce distractions. Think of an architect's large and ordered office, or the novelist Jonathan Franzen's injunction to write on a computer disconnected from the internet, the better to focus on the task at hand.

Lagerfeld's jumble is a corrective to this maxim. His clutter was the expression of the roaming, polyglot mind of a man whose hunger for the new never left him over his 70-year career. The mistake people make is to confuse untidiness with slovenliness, but there is a world of difference between a teenager's bedroom and the eccentric maximalism of the Sir John Soane's Museum in London, for example.[1] Living is a process of accumulation—of habits, memories and stuff—and there is a fine line between rubbish and treasure.

Even Marie Kondo, the interiors expert famed for her ruthless minimalism, has relaxed her stance, announcing earlier this year that she had "kind of given up" on tidying at home. Her motto was always that we should keep only those things that "spark joy," but surely those with an open mind would find the joy innate in any number of things. And if creativity is the interplay of different thoughts and ideas, why would you not have as many of them as close at hand as possible? The world is cluttered, whether it is visible in your office or not, and any successful path through it means managing a certain amount of chaos.

(1) Sir John Soane was one of the foremost architects of the Regency era in the UK. His central London home—crammed full of antiquities, furniture, sculptures, architectural models and paintings—has been preserved exactly as it was at the time of his death in 1837.

KINFOLK
NOTES

A new line of home and beauty products by *Kinfolk*, created to instil rituals and invite sensory pleasure into everyday life. Available at Kinfolk Dosan, Seoul.

CULT ROOMS

Words:
Stephanie d'Arc Taylor

The history— and future
—of Luna Luna Park.

A large-scale avant-garde art carnival—largely forgotten in the years since its 1987 debut in Hamburg—has been plucked out of obscurity by superstar rapper Drake and is currently being prepared for a comeback world tour. It's the coup of a lifetime for André Heller, the Austrian multimedia artist who brought the project to fruition more than 30 years ago and who has been haunted by its aborted promise ever since. The memory of Luna Luna, his name for the project, is "like a[n old] love affair where you can't stop having erotic dreams," he has previously said.

Every aspect of the resurrection saga reflects the fantastic, surreal qualities of the park's art installations, which were modeled after those that can be found in many regular Luna Park amusement parks around the world. To start with, it's an astonishing feat that Heller persuaded 30 of the most celebrated artists of the 20th century to create working carnival rides that were enjoyed by the hoi polloi usually left cold by high art. Compensation—just $10,000—was a fraction of their normal fees.[1]

At the time, the German magazine *Der Spiegel* attributed Heller's charm to a particular style of subtle, dark Viennese humor, known in German as *Wiener Schmäh*. Whatever he was doing seemed to work: The experimental American musician John Cage was the only artist who turned Heller down. The names of those who agreed to take part ring out: Keith Haring contributed a carousel, and Salvador Dalí a mirrored fun house. Carnival-goers rode a Ferris wheel painted by Jean-Michel Basquiat, accompanied by a Miles Davis song. Philip Glass also composed an original soundtrack to accompany a glass labyrinth by Roy Lichtenstein, and David Hockney created a musical "enchanted tree." Dazzled by the boldface names, Andy Warhol wanted to participate as well, but the other American artists involved objected to his inclusion, citing what they perceived as his crass late-career interest in profit.

Hailed by critics as a brilliant success, the show drew more than 250,000 attendees throughout the summer of 1987. Heller dreamed of a tour—of the world as well as of

Photo: © Luna Luna. Aerial view of Luna Luna, Hamburg, Germany, 1587.

"the suns and the moons"—but the exhibition soon fell into a bureaucratic morass where it was to languish for decades. In 2007, without a buyer or a clear legal path forward, the exhibition ended up in a storage unit in rural Texas.

Over a decade later, something stirred in the zeitgeist. In 2019, Heller heard from three different art world characters interested in resurrecting Luna Luna. There was a catch, aside from the multimillion dollar asking price: One of Heller's conditions was that the contents of the storage units were to be bought as-is, sight unseen. When Heller learned that Drake was interested, he did a deep dive into the rapper—"listening to his music, watching his attitudes," Heller has said.

The deal went through. For a reported $100 million, Drake's company, DreamCrew, was the owner of 44 shipping containers no one had looked into for over a decade. They lucked out: Not only were the artworks intact and largely undamaged, but there was original merch—posters and T-shirts designed by the artists.

Luna Luna is now being revitalized and reassembled in a warehouse in Los Angeles, and in the coming years, it will finally embark on the world tour Heller envisaged nearly 40 years ago. But he won't be at the helm. After it came out that he had repurposed Basquiat drawings and passed them off as originals, Heller stepped away from the project.

Perhaps it doesn't matter. Luna Luna has never been about Heller, just as it's not about Drake now. It's about the power of experiential art, celebrity and a unique view into the legacy of some of the artists who created the aesthetic world we live in today.

(1) In 1985, Heller received a grant of about $350,000 from the German magazine *Neue Revue* for the project. "The number of artistic movements it covers is kind of crazy," Kathy Noble, the curatorial director of the new Luna Luna, told *The New York Times* last year. "Everything from abstraction, art brut, Dada, Fluxus, Neo-Expressionism, nouveau realism, pop art, surrealism, Viennese Actionism—most exhibitions will not cover this breadth."

DIRECTORY

Photo: Marsý Hild Þórsdóttir

BEHIND THE SCENES

Words: Kabelo Sandile Motsoeneng

AOIFE MCMAHON on the art of the audiobook.

Aoife McMahon believes that artists deserve fair compensation for their labor. McMahon has performed across all mediums—on screen, radio and stage—and, having recorded over 200, has probably narrated your favorite audiobook too. For McMahon and numerous artists, each audiobook performance is a "vocal marathon" in which "you feel like you're in a one-woman play with 40 different characters."

Speaking on the phone from London, where she owns a recording studio that helps independent artists control the distribution of their work, McMahon describes her rigorous approach to narration and the changes she'd like to see in the industry.

KABELO SANDILE MOTSOENENG: Can you tell me about your journey to acting and audiobook performance?

AOIFE MCMAHON: I became an actress through quite a circuitous route. I actually started off in art school: I was working for small theater companies, and I had a big argument with my then boyfriend. He said, "If you want to be an actress, why don't you go and be an actress?" I marched off and phoned a drama school. The only name that popped in my head was RADA [Royal Academy of Dramatic Art] in London. I got an application, and the rest is history.

KSM: What elements of your training have been useful as you shifted mediums?

AM: The whole training concentrated on character, storytelling and truth. But specifically for audiobooks, we did radio training [and focused] on voice, mic techniques, radio plays and drama. Another aspect that was surprisingly useful was Shakespeare.

KSM: How is Shakespeare pertinent?

AM: The training is useful to be able to truthfully express human emotion and then turn it around quickly. In a Shakespeare play, you can go from ecstatic love to rage in one line. That's helpful for audiobooks where you're playing multiple characters and then have to come back into neutral narration.

KSM: How do you prepare for your audiobook projects?

AM: You kind of do it forensically; you're searching like a detective for any clues as to [the characters'] background, their education, whether they've traveled or not. Then you look for physical things, something that might give you a sharper voice. If you have several characters who are the same age, you think, *Well, can I change the accent of one of them?* Those things are based on what the writer has left for you along the way, those little breadcrumbs, but sometimes you make an executive decision.

KSM: How long does that work take?

AM: It depends on the length of the book, but generally three to four days. I do yoga sequences and vocal warm-ups like a singer so I can access those high notes for older people and the low notes for male characters.

KSM: What are some of the things you wish your industry could do away with?

AM: I'd like to do away with violence against women being used as entertainment. There's an awful lot of it out there. I've come across some where I'm thinking, *I'm uncomfortable with this.* I'm proud of the shift in female authors being brave and honest—not pretty and cute and compliant—when they use their voices to tell their stories.

KSM: And on the business side?

AM: I think the structure is unfair in how we're paid. We're paid per published hour—and if a book sells millions, that's it, there are no royalties.[1] It would be fair if there were royalties after a certain profit point. Not every book is going to afford anything except to publish itself, but then there are massive hits and the artists involved don't get remunerated the same way you would if you did a TV advert or a series or a film. It comes down to money, I'm afraid.

(1) McMahon is the narrator of all three audiobook versions of Irish author Sally Rooney's bestselling novels, *Conversations with Friends*, *Normal People* and *Beautiful World, Where Are You?*

CREDITS

COVER:	PHOTOGRAPHER	Zhong Lin
	STYLIST	Chen Yu
	HAIR	Juno Ko
	SET DESIGN	Yu Ting Tung
	CREATIVE PRODUCER	Vincent Wong
	MODEL	Sofi wears a necklace by MELTED POTATO and a ribbon and earring by MOTOGUO.
MAMOUDOU ATHIE:	FIRST ASSISTANT	Ben Joseph
	SECOND ASSISTANT	Neil Kanal
	STYLING ASSISTANT	Christina Ray
	STUDIO	Edge Studios
A WORLD OF DIFFERENCE:	ASSISTANTS	Zoe Zou & Haonan
URBAN DOOM:	CREATIVE PRODUCER	Vincent Wong
	PHOTO MANAGER	Daephen Foo
	FIRST PHOTOGRAPHY ASSISTANT	Yuan Ling Wang
	PHOTOGRAPHY ASSISTANTS	Yinghan Wang and Sherry Liu
	STYLING ASSISTANT	Yi Chuang
	MAKEUP ASSISTANT	Chloe Lai
	HAIR ASSISTANT	Anting Hsiao
	MODELS	Peng, Sofi, Asher, Dan and Wahcee
AMALIE SMITH:	LOCATION	Stevns Klint Experience
TOVE LO:	PHOTO ASSISTANTS	Justin Brooks & Patrick Molina
	DIGITAL TECHNICIAN	Mikayla Miller
KARIN MAMMA ANDERSSON:	PHOTOGRAPHY ASSISTANT	Hinke Tovle
	STYLING ASSISTANT	Hanna Svensson
FARES FARES:	STYLING ASSISTANT	Bella Sundström
SPECIAL THANKS:		Hôtel Martinez
		Harriet Fitch Little
		Siri Leijonhufvud
		Lincoln Robbin-Coker

STOCKISTS
A — Z

A	ACNE STUDIOS	acnestudios.com
	ADVISORY BOARD CRYSTALS	advisoryboardcrystals.com
	AERON	aeron.com
	ALAÏA	maison-alaia.com
B	BALENCIAGA	balenciaga.com
	BEPOSITIVE	bepositive.it
	BILLI BI	billibi.com
	BIRROT	birrot.com
	BOTTEGA VENETA	bottegaveneta.com
	BURBERRY	burberry.com
C	CARL HANSEN & SØN	carlhansen.com
	CDLP	cdlp.com
	COPERNI	coperniparis.com
	COURRÈGES	courreges.com
D	DSQUARED2	dsquared2.com
E	EYTYS	eytys.com
F	FARIS	farisfaris.com
	FERRAGAMO	ferragamo.com
G	GANT	gant.com
	GENTLE MONSTER	gentlemonster.com
	GUCCI	gucci.com
H	H&M	hm.com
	HERMÈS	hermes.com
	HOMME PLISSÉ ISSEY MIYAKE	isseymiyake.com
	HOPE	hope-sthlm.com
	HOUSE OF FINN JUHL	finnjuhl.com
	HUGO BOSS	hugoboss.com
I	IRO	iroparis.com
	ISABEL MARANT	isabelmarant.com
J	J. HANNAH	jhannahjewelry.com
	J. LINDEBERG	jlindeberg.com
	JEANERICA	jeanerica.com
	JOHN ELLIOTT	johnelliott.com
	JW ANDERSON	jwanderson.com
K	KENZO	kenzo.com
	KING & TUCKFIELD	kingandtuckfield.com
L	LOEWE	loewe.com
	LOUIS VUITTON	louisvuitton.com
	LOVECHILD 1979	lovechild1979.com
	LUCA FALONI	lucafaloni.com
M	MAISON MARGIELA	maisonmargiela.com
	MARC JACOBS	marcjacobs.com
	MARK KENLY DOMINO TAN	mkdtstudio.com
	MARSET	marset.com
	MEHROTRA	mehrotrasthlm.com
	MELITTA BAUMEISTER	melittabaumeister.com
	MELTED POTATO	meltedpotato.com
	MIU MIU	miumiu.com
	MOTOGUO	motoguo.com
	MUGLER	mugler.com
	MUJI	muji.com
N	NORDSTROM	nordstrom.com
O	OMEGA	omegawatches.com
	OUR LEGACY	ourlegacy.com
P	PANCONESI	marcopanconesi.com
	PAS UNE MARQUE	pasunemarqueparis.com
	PRADA	prada.com
	PYRRHA	pyrrha.com
S	SEAN SUEN	seansuen.com
	SLOTH ROUSING	slothrousing.com
	SOPHIE BUHAI	sophiebuhai.com
	STENSTRÖMS	stenstroms.com
	STRING FURNITURE	stringfurniture.com
T	TEURN STUDIOS	teurnstudios.com
	TINA FREY	tf.design
U	UNNA	unna.com
V	VIPP	vipp.com
W	WE11DONE	we11-done.com
	WELLIPETS	wellipets.com
X	XANDER ZHOU	xanderzhou.com
	XIMONLEE	ximonlee.com

KINFOLK

MY FAVORITE THING

Words:
Alexandra Marvar

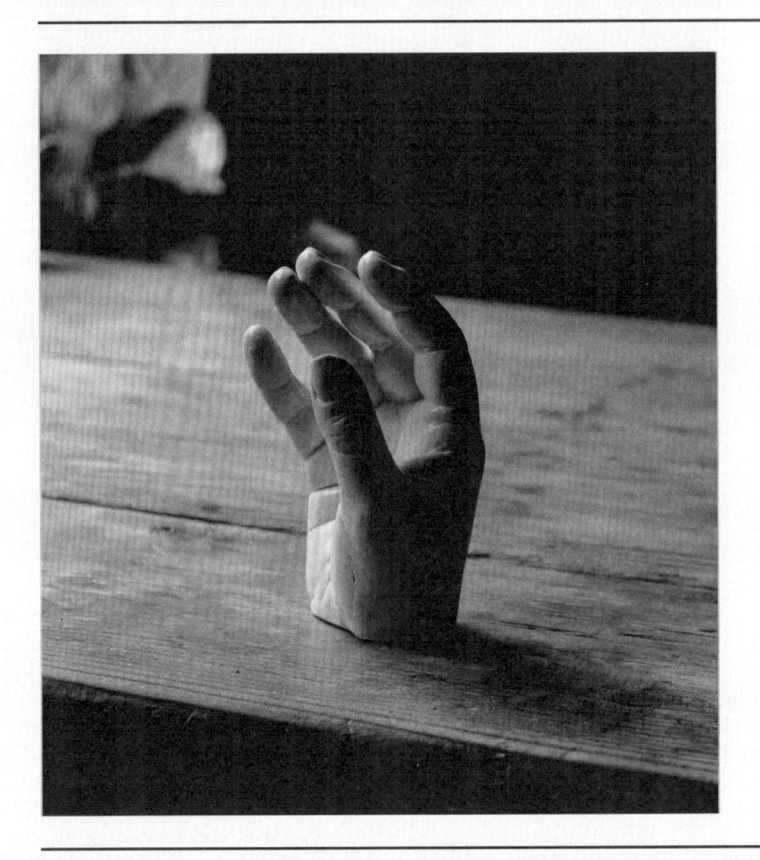

HEIDI GUSTAFSON, interviewed on page 66, on holding the hand of a faraway friend.

For my birthday this year, my best friend cast her own hand in plaster, so that I could hold it whenever I wanted to. So, this is the hand of my best friend, Devon Deimler. She's a mythologist, a scholar and an incredible artist, but she's been mostly a professor these days so it's meant a lot to me to see her artwork.

We went to art school in Baltimore together. Technically, we were in the sculpture department but it was more like social practice, following a lineage of conceptual artists, event-based artists. We were lucky. We had a rad professor. We had a bunch of people that would come down from New York—far-out thinkers.

We lived in Baltimore together for years, collaborating on many art projects. But ever since I moved up here [to Washington state] and she moved to LA—and with COVID— it's been hard to see each other. So, this gift of her hand was a very tender, loving one.

It can hold things, if I want it to. Or I can make offerings to her: *Oh, you're feeling depressed. Let me just rest a cigarette in here.* I have so many objects that are ancient, and so meaningful, in all different ways. This one is brand new to me. I love that freshness: Did not exist before. Created for me. It's just sweet. I mean: How often does a friend give you their hand?

—